ENCOURAGEMENT
HOW WORDS
CHANGE LIVES

Gordon Cheng

D1472286

Guidebooks for Life

Bible-based essentials
for your Christian journey

Encouragement is part of a series of straightforward,
practical Christian books from Matthias Media which
deal with the important nuts-and-bolts topics that
Christians need to know about as we walk each day
with our Master.

Some Christian books are all theory and no practical
application; others are all stories and tips with
no substance. The Guidebooks for Life aim to achieve a
vital balance—that is, to dig into the Bible and discover
what God is telling us there, as well as applying that
truth to our daily Christian lives.

For up-to-date information about the latest
Guidebooks for Life, visit our website:
www.matthiasmedia.com.au

GUIDEBOOKS FOR LIFE

ENCOURAGEMENT
HOW WORDS
CHANGE LIVES

Gordon Cheng

Encouragement: How Words Change Lives
© Matthias Media 2006

Matthias Media
(St Matthias Press Ltd. ACN 067 558 365)
PO Box 225
Kingsford NSW 2032 Australia
Telephone: (02) 9663 1478; international: +61-2-9663-1478
Facsimile: (02) 9663 3265; international: +61-2-9663-3265
Email: info@matthiasmedia.com.au
Internet: www.matthiasmedia.com.au

Matthias Media (USA)
Telephone: 724 964 8152; international: +1-724-964-8152
Facsimile: 724 964 8166; international: +1-724-964-8166
Email: sales@matthiasmedia.com
Internet: www.matthiasmedia.com

ISBN 978 921068 34 8

Cover design and typesetting by Lankshear Design Pty Ltd.

CONTENTS

TO FIONA

Chapter 1

WHAT CHRISTIAN ENCOURAGEMENT IS

I F YOU HAVE A NATURALLY SUNNY disposition, you will have picked up this book on encouragement and straight away thought, "Wonderful! This is exactly the sort of thing people need to read." You realize that you already are an encouraging person, and that this book will help you to do more of the same. Even though you don't need it yourself, you are drawn to it, in much the same way as an accountant is drawn to a book entitled *Make Your Life Add Up*, my wife is drawn to the garden on a sunny afternoon, and I am drawn to the worm farm when the pressure of life becomes too much to bear (hey, everyone needs something).

If, on the other hand, you have a more cynical cast of mind, you will be aware that 'encouragement' is one of the most over-used clichés ever to have arisen within Christian circles. You will suspect that a book about it is intended to make you work harder or feel worse, or probably both, and you have a suspicion that even the bits you agree with won't make much difference.

One of the difficulties for me in writing this book is that neither view is completely wrong. I do want happy, optimistic people to see that encouragement is something that flows naturally, under God, out of who we are. To that extent, this book confirms an idea you may already have sensed to be true. People who genuinely encourage other people are not putting it on. It comes out of who they are— or better, who God has made them.

On the other hand, it is also true that 'encouragement' is an over-used word whose meaning can be as vague as a bus driver's brain on a Monday morning. To urge people to 'be encouraging' is to add precisely nothing that might help them work out how to think and relate to others.

Myself, I can relate to the cynic very easily. Being the sort of individual who is able to see a cloud inside every silver lining, I naturally side with the person who expects absolutely nothing. I would expect a book on 'encouragement' to fit comfortably next to the one on the shelf entitled *Why You are a Miserable Failure and How My Expert Knowledge of You Might Help You Overcome This, at Which Point I Will Sell You Another Book.*

Which view does God endorse? In the end, you can see by the existence of this book that I've been convinced by the Bible that this subject really matters, and matters enough to ask both types of reader to read

on. I am not simply out to convince the naturally optimistic and happy person to keep using their innate gifts
to make others feel better. Nor do I want to cajole the
gloomy individual into trying a bit harder to say and do
slightly awkward or uncharacteristic things in order to
have an impact on others—even though either outcome
might actually be a good thing.

I have a bigger aim than this. I want to change what
you think about encouragement, about what it means
and how important it is. I want to convince you that
'encouragement' belongs to one of the most powerful
themes and ideas in the whole of Scripture. And that idea
is **the power of God's word to change lives**. I want to
show you that encouragement is not simply helping a
sad person feel happier, or a happier person to stay
happy. Rather, I am defining **Christian** encouragement
in this way:

> **Christian encouragement is speaking the truth
> in love**, with the aim of building Christians up in
> Christ-likeness, as we wait for the day of judgement.
> Christian encouragement will likewise involve
> speaking the truth in love to unbelievers, thus
> encouraging them to put their trust in Christ for
> forgiveness and salvation.

This idea of speaking the truth in love is taken straight
out of Ephesians 4:15, where Paul tells us Christ-like
maturity comes through us "speaking the truth in love"
to one another. The reminder about the day of judgement comes from Hebrews 10:25, where we are told that

we ought to be "encouraging one another, and all the more as you see the Day drawing near". "Speaking the truth in love" is an urgent task, because we are getting ready for the day of God's judgement.

Let's notice two things in this little phrase "speaking the truth in love". First, God tells us that we are to speak **the truth**. What we say to each other must line up with the facts as the Bible presents them. Those facts are found, first and foremost, in the gospel of Jesus Christ— the news about what God has done in Jesus' death and resurrection to bring forgiveness and make us God's children, so that we are now prepared to meet him on the final day of judgement and salvation.

The other thing to notice is that the speaking is done **in love**. Words can tear down, words can conceal or deceive or mislead, words can offer false comfort and false accusation. But if we really believe that truth can have an impact, we will want to speak in love, that is, with the good of the other person in mind, ahead of our own interests.

Notice that the aim of Christian encouragement— building people to Christ-likeness—fits perfectly with what God himself intends for us:

> And we know that for those who love God all things work together for good, for those who are called according to his purpose. For those whom he foreknew he also predestined to be conformed to the image of his Son, in order that he might be the firstborn among many brothers. (Rom 8:28-29)

God intends that we grow to be like Christ, and every

single event that happens to us should (and does) serve to advance this purpose of his. Speaking to each other is part of this.

Of course, this may or may not mean that we become happier individuals. Sometimes being conformed to the image of Christ will mean being disowned by family and friends, or putting strain on a marriage or a relationship. Also, some people are naturally sad. For them, being like Jesus may not improve their mood in a hurry. But the aim God has for us, happy or sad, is that we will indeed become like the one we have put our trust in. The Apostle Paul puts it like this:

> Indeed, I count everything as loss because of the surpassing worth of knowing Christ Jesus my Lord. For his sake I have suffered the loss of all things and count them as rubbish, in order that I may gain Christ and be found in him, not having a righteousness of my own that comes from the law, but that which comes through faith in Christ, the righteousness from God that depends on faith—that I may know him and the power of his resurrection, and may share his sufferings, becoming like him in his death, that by any means possible I may attain the resurrection from the dead. (Phil 3:8-11)

Note that Paul expects and wants to "share his sufferings" as a necessary part of becoming like Christ in his death and resurrection. My hope in this book is to persuade you to adopt this same aim as your own personal life-goal: the Christ-likeness of yourself and others. My prayer is that you'll see that this is not some-thing reserved for happy optimists or for professional Christians, ministers and Bible study leaders. It's for anyone who has been grabbed by the grace and glory of the gospel of Jesus.

Let's begin, then. Our investigation starts not with the broad notion of encouragement, but with a bit of thinking about speaking and the nature of words.

Chapter 2

THE POWER OF WORDS

CHRIS WAYNE,[1] IF YOU ARE reading this book I want you to know that you are a four-eyed son of a camel driver. You still owe me $2 million, and that's in 1975 money too!

Apologies to all other readers for that little outburst. A brief word of explanation: in 1975, I lent a small amount of money to Chris (yes, you, Chris) with a freely given promise from him (you) that he would give me back double the next day. If he didn't have it for me, then it would be double the day after, and so on until he paid back what he owed. Not being a Christian at the time, I had few moral qualms about the ethical implications of my usury (see Deut 23:19). But I did think, as I do now,

---

[1]   Throughout this book, some names have been changed to protect the innocent and, sometimes, the clearly guilty (that's you, Chris).

that people ought to keep their promises.

When I went back one week later, Chris owed me $6.40. Okay, not a large amount, but it was well over a week's allowance at the time. A week later when he still hadn't paid, the amount was $819.20. At the end of one month I said, "Come on, Chris, this is getting ridiculous. Let's just leave the debt you owe me at $2 million, and if you pay me that we can call it quits."

Now, I'm not really expecting to see even my original five cents returned at this late stage. I would like to think, maybe optimistically, that Chris's successful application to the New South Wales police force has taught him a bit more about ethical financial dealings. And yes, I admit too that my request for $2 million may have been a touch on the greedy side. But whatever the truth of the matter, I won't be pressing this one any further. Life is just like that sometimes.

Sometimes, however, misspoken words can represent much more than just a small annoyance. I know a man who was at his mother's side when she died in a hospital bed. Moments before she lost consciousness forever, she pulled him close and whispered to him two words: "You're adopted". It was a truth that hurt far more than many lies.

Words have impact. Consider the power of repeating words like these to children as they grow up:

- "You are a very clever child."
- "You are as clumsy as your uncle—in fact, worse!"
- "Well done."
- "Can't you stop bothering me?"

Even words spoken just once can make a difference. "I will", said in church in front of witnesses, can change two individuals and their families forever. In fact, every single word we speak has the potential to change ourselves and others. It's simply a matter of degree.

Empty words

All the same, many examples of how words are **not** powerful leap to mind. We can all think of cases where trusting what someone says has proven to be the exact opposite of a good idea.

A woman I know was told by her new boss that her existing job was perfectly safe. "You can stay as long as you like." Six months later her boss informed her that, despite good and faithful performance, this worker would soon be leaving the company. When the woman protested that the boss had given her word, the boss initially denied any such undertaking had been made, and then—unable to deny the facts due to the presence of witnesses—insisted vaguely that circumstances had changed, so that the first undertaking was no longer relevant. The boss admitted to feeling threatened by the ability and qualifications of her employee, and suggested that the loss of the job might prove to be the best thing for the woman. At any rate, said the boss, the intemperate way in which the woman had made her complaint about the matter had led to an irretrievable breakdown of relationship, and so in these new circumstances it would be impossible for the boss to keep her word. There was no union to appeal to, nothing had been placed in writing, and so the woman had no recourse. She lost her job and as a direct result was unable to keep living in her house.

Now such an example seems to be a classic demonstration that words are empty and useless. But a moment's reflection says that it was not the **words** that were the problem. Indeed, the words were of great comfort and reassurance to my acquaintance when she first heard them, and proved to be a real source of security, for a time. The words themselves were helpful and good. The problem was the person doing the speaking—in this case, a careless and dishonest boss. If this lady had thought before she'd spoken, she would not have spoken. But given that she did speak, and in fact made a promise, she should then have ensured that, despite personal inconvenience and difficulty, she remained true to what she had said. Had the boss been a Christian, she might well have been convicted by the words of Ecclesiastes:

> Pay what you vow. It is better that you should not vow than that you should vow and not pay. Let not your mouth lead you into sin, and do not say before the messenger that it was a mistake. (Eccl 5:4b-6a)

Our words express who we are. If our words are unreliable and devious, it is because **we** are unreliable and devious. If our words have power and integrity, that speaks volumes about our own integrity.

The book of Proverbs says a fair bit about this link between words and character. Proverbs 1:7 says, "The fear of the LORD is the beginning of knowledge; fools despise wisdom and instruction". Notice the contrast that is set up between two kinds of people with two very different characters: the one who wants to know many things and become wise begins by having a right fear of God; the basic characteristic of the fool, however, is that they don't listen to wisdom and instruction—they have no time for wise **words**.

This saying is so important that it is repeated in many different ways right through Proverbs. In Proverbs 9:10, the fear of the Lord is **the beginning of wisdom**; in Proverbs 15:33, the fear of the Lord is **instruction in wisdom**.

Here are some more verses from Proverbs that show this connection between words and character:

Words used for harm, spoken by people of foolish character	Words used for good, spoken by people of good character
Adulterers use words as traps for fools (Prov 7:10-21).	"The teaching of the wise is a fountain of life" (Prov 13:14).
"When words are many, transgression is not lacking" (Prov 10:19).	"The heart of the righteous ponders how to answer" (Prov 15:28)
"The words of the wicked lie in wait for blood" (Prov 12:6).	"... the mouth of the upright delivers them" (Prov 12:6).
There is one whose rash words are like sword thrusts" (Prov 12:18).	"... the tongue of the wise brings healing" (Prov 12:18).

Words used for harm, spoken by people of foolish character	Words used for good, spoken by people of good character
"The words of a whisperer are like delicious morsels; they go down into the inner parts of the body" (Prov 18:8).	"Gracious words are like a honeycomb, sweetness to the soul and health to the body" (Prov 16:24).
"Do you see a man who is hasty in his words? There is more hope for a fool than for him" (Prov 29:20).	"Whoever restrains his words has knowledge" (Prov 17:27).

Empty words don't reflect badly on the words themselves. They reflect on the character and integrity of the one doing the speaking. Words that fail or words that damage, therefore, reflect not so much on the nature of words as on the kind of people we are—sinful people who sin in what we think, in what we do, and in what we say. As Paul reminds the Romans:

> "None is righteous, no, not one ...
> Their throat is an open grave;
>   they use their tongues to deceive.
> The venom of asps is under their lips.
>   Their mouth is full of curses and bitterness."
> (Rom 3:10, 13-14)

Words that give life

Not all words are empty. Not all words fail.

1975 was a big year for me. Not only was I promised $2 million in cash that failed to materialize; this was also the year when Ian explained the gospel to me. It was not a flashy presentation. I saw no miracles, and Ian himself did nothing more than speak words to me. But as it happened, those words were life-changing.

Ian explained that being a Christian was quite simply a matter of life and death. He told me that if I trusted in Jesus rather than my own good deeds, I could be right with God, and that anyone who tried to be right with God through their own efforts was bound to fail. He explained that it was not a question of intellectual curiosity but of where I would spend eternity—heaven or hell.

I didn't believe a word he said.

All the same, I did agree with his logic when he suggested that there was a lot hanging on the right answers, and that I should find out more. So I started reading the Bible for myself. I considered the character of Jesus. I thought about what he said and the claims he made. And the more I thought about Jesus' words, the more extreme and offensive they seemed—unless, of course, they were true. "Whoever has seen me has seen the Father" (John 14:9). "I am the way, and the truth, and the life. No-one comes to the Father except through me" (John 14:6). "Whoever believes in the Son has eternal life; whoever does not obey the Son shall not see life, but the wrath of God remains on him " (John 3:36). "My son, your sins are forgiven" (Mark 2:5).

I was particularly grabbed by what Jesus taught about the human condition and our need for rescue. In one of his parables he compares humans to lost sheep, and himself to a shepherd who is searching for them. He leaves behind the 99 sheep who are okay, and goes off to search for the lost one. After much effort, he finds it and rescues it. "And when he comes home, he calls together his friends and his neighbours, saying to them, 'Rejoice with me, for I have found my sheep that was lost'" (Luke 15:6). I came to realize that we were all, myself included, trapped by sin and unable to please God. We were subject to his judgement, and the only way to escape from this 'lostness' was for him to rescue us. As I read and investigated further, I came to realize that Jesus was not just an exceptional man but God himself, in the form of a man, come to rescue me and forgive my sins.

The point is this: when I was persuaded enough by my friend's words to read the Bible, and then when I actually came to understand and trust those words I read in the Bible, God forgave me for all my sins. When I realized that Jesus Christ had come to seek and to save the lost; that I was one of those lost people; that his death on the cross was a death that I deserved but he took; and that through his life I could have life—everything changed. At the time, it felt a lot like thinking through some ideas that I was only vaguely familiar with, and hearing some words that I decided were trustworthy. In retrospect, that was the moment when I did what Jesus described when he said, "Truly, truly, I say to you, whoever hears my word and believes him who sent me has eternal life. He does not come into judgement, but has passed from death to life" (John 5:24).

This isn't just my story. **Anyone** who puts their trust in the words of Jesus has had this experience, and has passed over from death to life. These words of the gospel have enormous power. The Apostle Paul stakes his entire confidence in them when he says, "For I am not ashamed of the gospel, for it is the power of God for salvation to everyone who believes ..." (Rom 1:16).

A basic question, then, is whether or not **you** have experienced this power. Do you see yourself as, by nature, a sinner under God's judgement? If so, have you yet grasped that in Jesus' death, and because of God's love, you can be completely forgiven, and go from being God's enemy to being God's child?

Before reading this book any further, take time to sort this question out. Are you right with God? If not, read a Gospel[2] and find out how you can be forgiven. Find a friend who will explain it to you. Do some further homework and discover what the Bible says. And once it is clear in your mind that you **can** be forgiven by God, and that you **are** forgiven, take a moment to thank him for this amazing grace.

Once we have been convinced by the words of the gospel that sin can be forgiven, we don't need any further proof that words are powerful to change lives. Our own lives are the evidence that this is true. And why are these such powerful words? It is because ultimately the words of the gospel that we speak are not just our words, but the very words of God (1 Thess 2:13; cf. Prov 30:5).

Here is the real key to the power of words. God himself

---

[2] The Gospels are the books of Matthew, Mark, Luke and John in the Bible.

is a speaker. His words bring about change. He has made us speakers, and just as God speaks words that change lives, so also we—through our speaking—can change lives. In fact, that is the message of this book in a nutshell: **God's word changes us. Through us, it can change others too.**

So we can see this more clearly, we will now turn to consider the power and nature of the words that God speaks.

Chapter 3

THE GREATEST SPEAKER

OF COURSE WE STOOD UP. The fact that the Queen of Australia was not actually present was neither here nor there. We were Australian, and Queen Elizabeth was our Queen. And although—indeed **because**—it was 1965, "we did but see her passing by, yet we loved her till we died" (to slightly paraphrase our Prime Minister at the time). So it was enough that we were at the movies watching an orchestra on screen playing 'God Save the Queen', and we stood and paid our respects, before settling in for *Chitty Chitty Bang Bang*.

Australia was once part of the British Empire. That Empire was once powerful enough, even in its fading glory, to make us stand up in honour of it in a crowded movie theatre in George Street, Sydney, none of us doubting for a nanosecond that it was the perfect and right fulfilment of our duty.

Actually, that old Empire had power to do far more than pull us to our feet before a film. Here is Robert Menzies, Australian Prime Minister, speaking in 1939:

"It is my melancholy duty to inform you officially that, in consequence of a persistence by Germany in her invasion of Poland, Great Britain has declared war upon her, and that, as a result, Australia is also at war."[1]

With a single declaration, a **word**, spoken on the other side of the world, the nation of Australia (along with the British Commonwealth, much of Europe and eventually Asia and the United States) was drawn into a world war. The right person, speaking the right words at the right time, has immense power.

What I want to continue to do in this chapter is expand our appreciation of the power of words. In so doing, I want to completely blow apart (and in coming chapters, reconstruct) what it means for one person to offer encouragement to another. In order for this reconstruction to take place, some serious digging is needed. Like those colossal holes you sometimes see on city building sites, we will seem for a little bit to be doing hard work for little return. But if our biblical foundation is weak, the building we are working on won't stand. So we consider in this chapter not the words we say to each

---

[1]   The opening words of a speech given by Robert Menzies on 3 September 1939. A recording of these words can be heard at http://www.ww2australia.gov.au/wardeclared/index.html.

other, encouraging or otherwise, but the words of the first and greatest speaker of all.

RIGHT AT THE HEART of the power of words—and we have touched on this in Chapter 1—is the question of the character, integrity and power of the one who is speaking. The title of a recent book, *Lies and the Lying Liars Who Tell Them,* is not bad as a summary of this idea: if you lack integrity, your words will lack integrity.

But what if the speaker is God?

It won't cause any reader to fall off their chair in astonishment to learn that "God is not man, that he should lie, or a son of man, that he should change his mind" (Num 23:19). God's words are, at a conservative estimate, approximately 1,000,000% more powerful and effective than anything we might say. For starters, God tells no lies. But a great deal more can be said. Since God possesses infinite power, wisdom and knowledge, it follows that his **words** possess infinite power, wisdom and knowledge. It's impossible that they could be anything other than true, and capable of achieving what God intends.

> "For as the rain and the snow come down from heaven
>   and do not return there but water the earth,
> making it bring forth and sprout,
>   giving seed to the sower and bread to the eater,
> so shall my word be that goes out from my mouth;
>   it shall not return to me empty,
> but it shall accomplish that which I purpose,
>   and shall succeed in the thing for which I sent it."
> (Isa 55:10-11)

Let's think about just how powerful God's word is. Consider the moment of creation:

> In the beginning, God created the heavens and the earth. The earth was without form and void, and darkness was over the face of the deep. And the Spirit of God was hovering over the face of the waters. And God said, "Let there be light", and there was light. (Gen 1:1-3)

The role of God's word is to bring every single thing that exists into being. God "gives life to the dead and calls into existence the things that do not exist" (Rom 4:17).

Now even in human experience, we know that words can have power. There's something astounding, for example, about the fact that a British declaration of war could immediately involve every citizen of a country on the other side of the world in that same war. God's word is powerful in the same way, only more so. "By the word of the LORD the heavens were made, and by the breath of his mouth all their host" (Ps 33:6).

Here is the theologian and poet Bruce Smith reflecting on that psalm:

> These two lines of poetry, so starkly simple, are immortal. It seems to me an astonishing miracle that as I speak, the words on my mouth reflect the thoughts of my mind. It is extraordinary, this gift of speech that we have: that I am able to take the normal, unthinking, spontaneous process of breathing, and by subtle manoeuvres of air articulate my thoughts and project something from inside my mind to be taken possession of in yours. My breath

is essential: not only does it keep me going, it is also the vehicle by which I relate to you.

In the opening verses of Genesis we are told of a great dark and deep silence. Darkness is over everything; nothing is to be seen. There is total, impenetrable blackness. But the breath—the spirit— of God, is moving. The breathing of God, the life of God, is suddenly articulated, and those words ring out in the midst of darkness: Let there be light!

And immediately, in response to that word, light bursts onto creation.

More than this, he who made this world is he who maintains and sustains this world. It is an incredible thought. We are such a tiny part of the vast, massive, seething humanity that occupies this globe of ours. And yet our creator God sustains this creation in all its vastness, down to every level of molecular, atomic and subatomic activity. Not one infinitesimal part of the created order is not fully, consciously known to him. [2]

So we see God's word and God's Holy Spirit working together to achieve God's purposes. This pattern is repeated right through the Bible. Just as God's word and God's breath ('breath' equals 'spirit' in the original Hebrew) can't be separated when God speaks at creation, so both God's word and God's breath/Spirit continue to sustain that creation.

---

[2]   Bruce Smith, 'Living in this world', *kategoria*, 24, 2002, pp. 26-27.

Here is the sea, great and wide,
>   which teems with creatures innumerable,
>   living things both small and great.
There go the ships,
>   and Leviathan, which you formed to play in it.
These all look to you,
>   to give them their food in due season.
When you give it to them, they gather it up;
>   when you open your hand, they are filled with
>   good things.
When you hide your face, they are dismayed;
>   when you take away their breath, they die
>   and return to their dust.
When you send forth your Spirit, they are created,
>   and you renew the face of the ground. (Ps 104:25-30)

Some people think of God as a cosmic watchmaker, who made the universe and wound it up, and is now just letting it gradually wind down over eternity.[3] Every now and then God may take an interest in the doings of human beings, and stick his finger into the mechanism. This will cause a disturbance—perhaps a natural disaster, or sometimes a miracle—but then God will withdraw quickly and quietly back to doing nothing. But this is nothing like the God of the Bible.

In the Bible, God is present and active, and it shows in the power of his speaking.

---

[3] This view is often referred to as 'deism', the belief in an original creator 'god' who is now remote from his creation.

- He speaks to create and sustain.
- He speaks to command and bless.
- He speaks to judge.
- He speaks to promise.
- He speaks to reveal himself.
- He speaks in the gospel to save and transform those who hear him.

This is not a complete list. Indeed, every part of human experience and creation is shaped and addressed by God's word—from sex, to vegetarianism, to angels and demons, to politics and the affairs of nations, to the squishing of ants. Some of these things are talked about explicitly in the Bible. Others, like embryo cloning or computer technology or sunglasses, aren't mentioned directly, yet there are truths and principles in Scripture that apply directly to them. Nothing is too small for God. "Are not two sparrows sold for a penny? And not one of them will fall to the ground apart from your Father. But even the hairs of your head are all numbered" (Matt 10:29-30).

Through God's speaking of words, Adam and Eve become aware of who they are and what they are supposed to do within God's creation. They are to "be fruitful and multiply and fill the earth and subdue it and have dominion over the fish of the sea and over the birds of the heavens and over every living thing that moves on the earth" (Gen 1:28). God's word spells out the blessings of the garden, and the responsibilities that Adam and Eve (and their descendants—us!) have within God's world. God uses words to command obedience: "... of the tree of the knowledge of good and evil you shall not eat, for in the day that you eat of it you shall surely die" (Gen 2:17).

It's really not surprising, then, that the first assault against God is a direct attack on his word. "Did God actually say ... ?" questions the serpent in Genesis 3:1. He then distorts God's command in a way that suggests God is up to no good at all. "Did God actually say, 'You shall not eat of any tree in the garden'?"—to which the right answer is, or should have been, "Not even close". This is not what Eve says, however. She botches her answer and tells the snake a far harsher version of God's command than the one God actually gave. "You shall not eat of the fruit of the tree that is in the midst of the garden, neither shall you touch it", which is not quite as inaccurate as the snake, but is still a distortion. The snake moves from God's word to God's character. He questions God's goodness and his motives, and the rest (as they say) is history.

It's no wonder that one of Jesus' descriptions for Satan is the "father of lies" (John 8:44). We may, if we have watched the wrong sort of movies, associate satanic power with spinning heads and green vomit. The Bible, by contrast, sees that Satan's power consists in distorting and misrepresenting God's word to us—even the words of Scripture. When Satan tests Jesus in the wilderness, he does so with words and Bible verses. Jesus' response is likewise in the form of words, but with the words of Scripture **rightly applied**.

These observations about twisted and distorted words lead us straight into the dark side of God's words:

To the woman he said,

> "I will surely multiply your pain in childbearing;
>> in pain you shall bring forth children.
> Your desire shall be for your husband,
>> and he shall rule over you."

And to Adam he said,

> "Because you have listened to the voice of your wife
>> and have eaten of the tree
> of which I commanded you,
>> 'You shall not eat of it,'
> cursed is the ground because of you;
>> in pain you shall eat of it all the days of your life;
> thorns and thistles it shall bring forth for you;
>> and you shall eat the plants of the field.
> By the sweat of your face
>> you shall eat bread,
> till you return to the ground,
>> for out of it you were taken;
> for you are dust,
>> and to dust you shall return." (Gen 3:16-19)

These words follow on from the lies of the snake, and the subsequent disobedience of Adam and Eve in trusting the words of the snake rather than the words of God. Just as God's word creates the world and living things and orders their existence, now God's word undoes creation and brings death and disorder. God's word is the beginning of life but it is also the end of it. "You are dust, and to dust you shall return." Some words are devastating because they are lies. God's words are devastating for sinners like us because they are based on truth, justice and the power to carry out what is threatened. The sentence of death is God's verdict against us when we refuse to obey him and his command. The Apostle Paul has a succinct and painful summary of this situation: "The wages of sin is death" (Rom 6:23).

Like the other words of judgement in Genesis 3, God's punishment of the snake looks to the future. The woman and the snake will be enemies, and their offspring will continue to hurt each other. At one level, this is part of the judgement on the snake—that enmity between snakes and humans would be an ongoing feature of life after the Fall. But the judgement on the snake also raises our expectations. What will be the result of this ongoing hostility? Will the work of the snake, which was to lure humanity into rebellion against God, ever be thwarted? Will Eve's offspring ever escape the malign influence of the snake? Will they ever finally defeat the snake?

This expectation shapes just about everything that follows in the rest of the Bible. The creation has rebelled against its Creator, and suffered the consequences. What will God do about it? Will he be content to allow his creative purposes to be ruined? Will he allow the conflict between humanity and the serpent to go on forever?

As the Old Testament begins to unfold, God sets out to answer these questions by making promises—promises that will eventually lead to the restoration and renewal of the whole creation. Blessings will come through the family of one man, Abraham (Gen 12:1-3). They will centre on the nation Israel, and flow on to the whole world through this kingdom of priests (Exod 19:4-6). A king from the line of

David will sit on God's throne in Jerusalem forever (2 Sam 7:12-16). Jerusalem will be the place where God rules, and all nations will flow in to her to be blessed (Isa 2:2-4). God will renew his creation with a river of life flowing from his holy temple (Isa 65:17-25: Ezek 47:1-12). Sin will finally be dealt with, and God's people will know God and serve him willingly (Isa 52:13-53:12; Jer 31:31-34).

Sure enough, when we reach the New Testament we discover that every single promise God has made is kept in Christ. "For all the promises of God find their Yes in him" (2 Cor 1:20). At the cross, and in his rising from death, Jesus bears completely the punishment and anger of God against human sin; not just the sin of Adam in the garden, but the sin of all mankind. At the cross, and as a direct result of this dealing with sin, the age-old conflict between humanity and the snake is decisively ended. The ultimate Snake is defeated: "The reason the Son of God appeared was to destroy the works of the devil" (1 John 3:8).

That is, at the cross, the cause of all the damage done to God's perfect creation has been dealt with. We do not, as the New Testament reminds us constantly, see the world made perfect just yet. But we know that the root of the problem has been fixed. Consider this astounding verse from Paul:

> Therefore, if anyone is in Christ, he is a new creation.
> (2 Cor 5:17)

Anyone who trusts in Jesus is indeed a "new creation". Through Jesus' death and resurrection, our sins have been wiped out. We have been adopted by God and made his children. We have been given the Holy Spirit to change us into the likeness of Christ. And how has God brought this transformation about? It has all happened in and through the power of his word.

> For God, who said, "Let light shine out of darkness," has shone in our hearts to give the light of the knowledge of the glory of God in the face of Jesus Christ. (2 Cor 4:6)

That is a powerful word. The same God who spoke and brought creation into being now speaks, through the gospel, to bring a **new** creation into being. We are moved from death to life.

GOD IS THE GREATEST SPEAKER. Amazingly, through his speech, we also get to be speakers. God creates humans **"in his own image"** with the ability to use words, and considering the huge amount of power tied up with speaking, this is no small thing (Gen 1:26-27). Like God, we rule over creation, only under his authority. Alone of all creation, we get to speak with God and with each other, and in the process we establish relationships, and use our words to describe and control and shape creation.[4]

In our next chapter we will consider how God's word works through our words to transform others.

---

[4] One early hint of this is in Genesis 2, where the animals are named by us; we are not named by them. This summing up of their existence with a name reveals and hints at something of the greatness of human authority, and the power God has given to us in our speaking.

Chapter 4

How Christian Encouragement Works: Part 1

We know that God's words are powerful. But how does that power translate into the words we speak to each other? We know from experience that our words can also have the power to change lives. The question is, how? How does our encouragement of each other work?

At the most basic level, our words are able to encourage other people because, like God, we possess the power of language. God, the greatest speaker, made us to be speakers as well. Like him, we are relational in nature, and our relationships with each other are built on words. You can't know someone unless you speak to them, and they speak to you. And when we do speak, as we saw in Chapter 1, our words often have huge impact. "You're fired." "I love you." "I resign." "Yes, I will."

"You're adopted." "I promise to be there."

However, what is it about at least some of our speaking that gives it the quality of 'encouragement'? How does our speech gain the power to build people up?

How the gospel changes lives

One way to start answering this question is to think about the gospel, because the gospel is a very obvious instance of our words having great power. When we open our mouths and tell people about the coming judgement and the saving lordship of Jesus, we participate in transferring people from darkness to light, from death to life. The gospel is the power of God for salvation. We hear it and it saves us; we pass it on to others, and it saves them too. This is a very pure and obvious example of seeing our words change people's lives. If we can understand what is going on at this point—when we speak the gospel to someone—then it should be straightforward to work out how other forms of Christian encouragement work as well.

There's another good reason to start our investigation into how encouragement works by thinking about the gospel. Although encouragement covers a great multitude of different ways of speaking, when we consider **Christian** encouragement we are not talking about helping someone feel happy and stay happy, but about building them up in Christ-likeness, as we discussed in Chapter 1. In this context, speaking the gospel to someone is basic. It's not possible for someone to become truly Christ-like until they have trusted him for the forgiveness

of their sins through the gospel, and begun to acknowledge that Jesus is their Lord. Any other encouragement
that we offer is going to build on the gospel.

So then, let's work through step by step so that we
can see how the gospel changes lives.

The gospel was spoken first by God. At its most basic
level, it is the message that Jesus is the ruler of God's
kingdom, and that through his death on the cross and his
rising from the dead, we can avoid the judgement we
deserve for ignoring him. We do this by putting our trust
in him and asking his forgiveness. When we acknowledge
Jesus as not only the ruler of God's kingdom but **our** king,
we are forgiven and begin to enjoy the glorious benefits of
relationship with him forever.

This gospel was promised in the Old Testament to
Abraham and the prophets, and then revealed fully in
Jesus who "came into Galilee, proclaiming the gospel of
God" (Mark 1:14). We can now 'hear' this gospel of God
in one of two ways. Either we can read it for ourselves
(in the Bible), or someone can tell us. And it is through
this hearing of the gospel that God works to change us.

Sometimes this hearing can come about in surprising
ways. I know a man who was returning home from the
pub, drunk. For reasons best known to himself, he
climbed into an electricity substation, was subsequently
blasted by 25,000 volts, and woke some time later in
hospital. Bored in his hospital bed, and challenged by a
friend to sort his life out, he picked up a Bible, began to
read Paul's letter to the Romans, and right there and then
decided that he needed to become a Christian.

Normally, people come to know the gospel in less exciting circumstances. But we mustn't ever lose sight of how significant this moment of hearing the gospel really is. Someone hears the message. They are transformed by it—and so they pass from death to life, and it has effects on their character, their way of living, and their ways of relating to others. Next, they tell others that message. Those people in turn hear it, understand it, and likewise pass over from death to life. They too change in their character, their way of living and their ways of relating to others. Paul in his first letter to the Thessalonians gives a wonderfully short and simple description of how this happened in their case:

> For we know, brothers loved by God, that he has
> chosen you, because our gospel came to you not only
> in word, but also in power and in the Holy Spirit and
> with full conviction. (1 Thess 1:4-5)

The Thessalonians were changed completely; the gospel came to them "not only in word". When the gospel really hits, that is a work of God's Holy Spirit, Paul insists.

This is a crucial point. God's word and God's Spirit work together in the very closest of harmony—as someone has said, God's word and God's Spirit are like his right and left hand. They work together to bring change.

Some Christians respect God's word, but don't realize that the reason it's so powerful is that God's Spirit takes the word and applies it to our lives. If that wasn't so, then reading the Bible would be a bit like reading a powerful speech or a favourite story—impressive and enjoyable, but not powerfully life-changing in the way reading the Bible or hearing its message is for Christians. The Spirit uses God's word, the Bible, to bring us from death to life. And the Spirit uses Christians who speak that same message to change others, too.

Jesus explains the link between God's Spirit and God's word to his disciples like this: "the Helper, the Holy Spirit, whom the Father will send in my name, he will teach you all things and bring to your remembrance all that I have said to you" (John 14:26). The key word here is "remembrance". The Holy Spirit won't say or teach anything separate or different from what Jesus has already said and taught, "for he will not speak on his own authority, but whatever he hears he will speak, and he will declare to you the things that are to come" (John 16:13). So the Holy Spirit won't be revealing to us the cure for cancer, or the name of the person we will marry, or the future price of Microsoft shares. The Holy Spirit will be teaching us about Jesus—and indeed, that is exactly what the disciples who heard Jesus speak were helped to do.

This work of God's word and Spirit is far more effective in producing permanent change in someone's life than 25,000 volts to the body. And so the Thessalonians are described just a few verses later as having turned "from idols to serve the living and true God". In a culture where idols were thought to represent real spiritual forces, and completely dominated every aspect of life—eating, drinking, sex, commerce, travel, home life —this small phrase of Paul's suggests an extraordinary turnaround.

Of course, we know as Christians that such extraordinary change was not limited to first-century Thessalonica. This change in people's lives has been happening ever since, and it's not hard to find examples, either in history or in personal experience.

There have been people like Jack, the 80-year-old man I met in a church on Sydney's North Shore. The very first time I turned up at that church, some 20 years ago, Jack introduced himself to me. Actually, that in itself is a sign of the grace of God! There are very few places in the world outside church where friendships form easily and naturally between people of completely different ages, races, temperaments, interests and upbringing. Yet in churches throughout the world, people from very different backgrounds—often traditionally hostile to each other—can be found worshipping the same God together.

Jack told me in that first conversation that years earlier he had got down on his knees in desperation and prayed to the God he hadn't believed in (until then) to turn his marriage around from the brink of divorce. Forty-five years later he and his wife were still together, and still going strong in their Christian faith. And he was there in church welcoming people that he'd never set eyes on before, and helping them to feel comfortable there.

Arthur's life changed because of the gospel too. Fortunately or unfortunately, depending on your side of the case, he became noticeably less effective as a lawyer when he became a Christian. He stopped lying and cheating and aggressively getting away with anything he could in order to win court cases, and instead began to act with integrity and honesty, treating even opposing counsels with honour and respect (mind you, as a lawyer he is still not what you would call 'cuddly').

It happened to Zoe, who worked as a nurse in an African hospital but realized that, for all her good works and self-sacrificial service of others, she still didn't have the peace of mind and purpose in life that her Christian colleagues had. The externals of her life were in order, but she found that she had no contentment at all, until the day she put her trust in Jesus.

It happened to Evan, whose work in the finance industry could have seen him living in a large house in any suburb in Sydney, one of the most prosperous and comfortable cities in the world. Instead, to the amazement of his colleagues, he chose to live in a far more modest house close to a good local church, so that he could give more of his money to gospel work.

It happened to Lee, who was addicted to gambling, alcohol, masturbation and pornography. On hearing the gospel and trusting it, he repented of his lifestyle, married, had children and started to attend his local church regularly, all the while praying that God would work in him. God sorted him out, and he now runs a small business and is an elder in his local church.

Because of God's Holy Spirit, the spoken word of the gospel is accompanied by massive change. Usually that change is obvious to anyone who knows the person. Notice how Paul describes this work of God's Spirit through his word as flowing on beyond the Thessalonians:

And you became imitators of us and of the Lord, for you received the word in much affliction, with the joy of the Holy Spirit, so that you became an example to all the believers in Macedonia and in Achaia. For not only has the word of the Lord sounded forth from you in Macedonia and Achaia, but your faith in God has gone forth everywhere, so that we need not say anything. (1 Thess 1:6-8)

The gospel word didn't stop with the first group of hearers (in this case, the Thessalonians), but flowed on to others. We could trace this out in both directions—back to Jesus, and forward from the Thessalonians:

> First Jesus proclaims the gospel
> (e.g. Mark 1:14)

▼

> then Paul is transformed from murderer to messenger when he meets the risen Jesus and hears him speak
> (Acts 9)

▼

> then the Thessalonians are changed from idolaters to people waiting for Jesus' return when they hear the gospel from Paul
> (1 Thess 1:9-10; see a spectacular parallel in Acts 19:17-41)

▼

> then everyone in Macedonia and Achaia
> hears about this transformation. They in turn are
> affected by the gospel word.

▼

> The gospel is spoken from country to country and from
> generation to generation.

▼

> Today, we hear this same gospel that was heard
> and passed on by the Thessalonians. Because of the
> Holy Spirit, we respond just as they did, turning from
> our idols to serve God.

Same story, different angle

The Thessalonians were not some freak of ancient history. Here's a different angle on the same process, this time from the fourth chapter of Paul's letter to the Ephesian Christians. Here, the focus is on how the Lord Jesus Christ himself enables and oversees the powerful work of God's word through us:

> Therefore it says,
>> "When he ascended on high he led a host of captives,
>>   and he gave gifts to men".
> (In saying, "He ascended", what does it mean but that
> he had also descended into the lower parts of the earth?
> He who descended is the one who also ascended far
> above all the heavens, that he might fill all things.)
> (Eph 4:8-10)

This is a description of the impact of the word of the gospel, seen this time from the perspective of the work of the risen Christ. Jesus became a man ("descended") and died for sins. Afterwards, he "ascended"—he rose from the dead, having defeated sin and bought our redemption by the price of his blood.

But that's not all! What happens next is very significant for understanding the way the gospel continues to have an impact. "He gave gifts to men", says Paul. What were those gifts?

> And he gave the apostles, the prophets, the
> evangelists, the pastor-teachers,[1] to equip the saints
> for the work of ministry, for building up the body of
> Christ, until we all attain to the unity of the faith and
> of the knowledge of the Son of God, to mature
> manhood, to the measure of the stature of the
> fullness of Christ ... (Eph 4:11-13)

The image here would have been very familiar—possibly too familiar—for readers under the Roman empire in the first century. It's a picture of a glorious military victory procession. The enemy has been crushed. The victorious general returns with his army, bringing with him humiliated prisoners chained and harassed. In the course of the victory procession, the winner of the military contest (Jesus, who has triumphed over death) is seen handing out the spoils of battle to the watching crowd. In this case, the

---

[1]   ESV margin.

gifts he gives are people. They are people that he has 'won' through his great victory, and he now distributes these prizes to the cheering crowds.

It is fascinating that the particular people mentioned as gifts to the church—apostles, prophets, evangelists, pastor-teachers—are all, every single one of them, speakers of God's word. Apostles and prophets are those responsible for the speaking and writing of the Bible. Evangelists have the job of announcing the gospel word to the world. Pastor-teachers explain God's word, maybe one-to-one, maybe in a church.[2]

And when all these speakers speak, what happens next? Ephesians 4 rounds out the picture. Their speaking equips us (that is Christians, members of the church) ...

> ... so that we may no longer be children, tossed to and
> fro by the waves and carried about by every wind of
> doctrine, by human cunning, by craftiness in deceitful
> schemes. Rather, speaking the truth in love, we are to
> grow up in every way into him who is the head, into
> Christ, from whom the whole body, joined and held
> together by every joint with which it is equipped,
> when each part is working properly, makes the body
> grow so that it builds itself up in love. (Eph 4:14-16)

What ought to strike us from these verses is that **every single Christian** gets to speak. No-one misses out. There

---

[2]   For more detail on this passage, see P. T. O'Brien's excellent Ephesians commentary in the *Pillar* series (Eerdmans, Grand Rapids, 1999).

is no sense of any individual getting a free pass to go and sleep in the corner while the apostles and prophets and all the other specialists do what they're supposed to do, building the church. The church is not meant to consist of a few expert speakers speaking God's word, while the rest of us work at our day jobs or organize church building programmes or morning teas (without in the least wanting to denigrate day jobs, morning teas or building programmes; well, not all of them, anyway). Anyone who is part of the body of Christ will, without any exception, be "speaking the truth in love" so as to bring the body to maturity.

It follows that there is something deeply unnatural about being a Christian and wanting to keep your faith to yourself. Anyone who belongs to Christ and has been swept up in his victory over sin and death will long to see others share the fruits of that victory, and so will open their mouths to tell others of the great things Christ has done. To use an analogy, there is not a percussionist in any orchestra in the entire Western world who does not long for that part of the symphony where the conductor points at them, and they get to go 'Ting!' with their triangle.

Or, to use an example from sport rather than music, there isn't a soccer player in the game who wouldn't like to be wearing the boot that kicks the ball that scores the goal that humiliates the opponent, wins the final, restores national pride and so causes a turnaround in the economy that funds the research that finds the cure for cancer. Even the goalie would love to have a go, given the opportunity.

All right, there may be just a hint of exaggeration here. But in exactly the same way, Christians who really understand the gospel that has saved us simply love to speak about it, and will grab any opportunity to tell of the wonderful things Jesus has done for them.

I hope that if you are reading this book and realize just how wonderful it is to belong to Christ, you will become not noisy, not objectionable, not offensive—but just someone who will be very difficult to shut up when it comes to your favourite topic: how wonderful it is to be forgiven and to belong to the Lord Jesus by faith.

God's fellow workers

Once we understand all this, we can begin to rejoice in the privilege of being God's fellow workers. Here is what Paul says about this when he writes to the bitterly divided Corinthian Christians:

> What then is Apollos? What is Paul? Servants through
> whom you believed, as the Lord assigned to each.
> I planted, Apollos watered, but God gave the growth.
> So neither he who plants nor he who waters is
> anything, but only God who gives the growth. He who
> plants and he who waters are one, and each will
> receive his wages according to his labour. For we are
> God's fellow workers ... (1 Cor 3:5-9)

In describing his ministry (and that of Apollos) in this way, Paul is ruling out any boasting or status-seeking by Christian ministers, and offering a rebuke to the fractious

Corinthians. As he does so, Paul reveals something very important about our ministry to one another. As we **speak the truth in love** to one another, we are working alongside God himself. We are planting and watering, but God through his Holy Spirit is giving the growth. Unless God's Holy Spirit opens the heart of the person to hear and receive the message, our words will be useless—no matter how true they are, or how cleverly we express them. We can't reach inside a person and change their heart for them. God's Spirit can. As he does so, the word can take root and grow and lead to changed lives. We are **fellow workers with God**.

This is an incredible privilege, and also a great reassurance for the anxious. We may be very hesitant about our own ability. We may be convinced that we will fail in both word and action. Even if we don't think this of ourselves, it is quite likely that we will look around at church and think it about Myrtle, Ethel or Patrick. We may be only too aware of the weaknesses of the denomination or Christian organization we belong to, or of the leaders in our own congregation. It is very reassuring and encouraging to recognize that **God** is our fellow worker, and that **he** will give the growth. God's Holy Spirit will take our poor, weak words and use them with great power in the hearts, minds and lives of our hearers.

It is like gardening (or at least gardening in the Cheng household). When the entire family decides to plant baby lettuce on a Saturday afternoon in the backyard, certain realities apply and certain home truths about family dynamics and gardening knowledge must be taken into account. My wife is extremely well aware of these realities; the rest of us are somewhat aware in a descending order that begins with me, and gradually drops down to our seven-year-old (who, truth be known, is starting to get quite good and is beginning to ask questions about my ability in this area), down to our four-year-old and finally to our three-year-old. The latter two contribute enthusiasm and a certain degree of, let's say, unrestrained passion about how things ought to be done and who ought to do them first. As a direct result of this scenario, it is fair to suggest that every single task that needs to be completed in the garden takes three to five times longer than if Fiona (my wife) were to do it herself. Digging a furrow takes longer. Putting plants into the furrow takes longer. It is an activity fraught with risk both to the baby lettuce and to the dogs underfoot. At least one adult is employed for the entire gardening period keeping an eye on the most recent location of the pitchfork, and helping recover small plants from under a layer of newly thrown mulch. Snails, as the oldest of us have now realized, are not potential pets—but we haven't yet had the heart to tell the two youngest, and so the location of their mollusc collection has also turned out to be one of those things that just has to be carefully monitored.

But for all the slow, distracting and sometimes dangerous things that happen in our garden, there is no doubt that all of us **really are gardening**. Every single one of the children's mistakes, and a good number of mine as well, will be overruled by grace. The good things we do **really are** good things. In the kindness and providence of God, the children (and I) are becoming better gardeners than when we first began. When we stand in the garden in the summer sunshine we will be happy, because **we really did it**.

And that is how it is with God and us, his fellow workers, in his church. We really are helping him. Those who see our efforts may laugh at what we do. We ourselves may become frustrated and upset by mistakes and lack of competence. We may become dimly aware, from time to time, that what we thought was useful and helpful was, unfortunately, nothing of the sort. But provided that we keep our focus on what God says in his word, and continue to speak that same truth in love, the gospel we speak will continue to transform our own lives and the lives of others. And that gospel work will result in a growth that bears fruit into eternity.

> For what is our hope or joy or crown of boasting before our Lord Jesus at his coming? Is it not you? For you are our glory and joy. (1 Thess 2:19-20)

Chapter 5

How Christian encouragement works: Part II

Gospel words are obviously powerful. As we saw in our last chapter, when the gospel of Jesus' death and resurrection is spoken to us and God's Spirit is working in us, we are transformed; and in turn, we have the privilege of speaking that gospel word to others, who are also thus transformed.

Gospel words are not the only words we speak as Christians, however. Our encouragement of others is founded upon the gospel, but it doesn't stop there. In this chapter, we look at two other sorts of Christian speaking: words of wisdom, and words of prayer.

Words of wisdom

Suppose I know you, and know something of what you've been up to recently. Suppose I tell you that the time and effort you put into building that cubby house for your nephews was hugely appreciated. I happen to know (and I tell you so) that they love it so much that they are virtually living in it on weekends, and are pestering their parents to let them set up a TV and a pool table out there.

Now in passing on this happy news, I haven't told you the gospel—but it's pretty obvious that I have encouraged you. Or to think of quite a different example, if I summon up the courage to ask how you are coping after the death of your sister, and empathize with you by sharing how I felt after the death of a close relative, there is little doubt that what I have done is also perfectly consistent with Christian encouragement.

How should we think about what is going on here? After all, the words are not specifically Christian. There's no gospel in them whatsoever. Words of encouragement like this could just as easily have been spoken by my friend the atheist photographer—the one who keeps his son away from school scripture classes because it's 'baloney', and who makes sure that at age seven, he reads books about the Greek and Roman gods of mythology so that his education will be complete.

Realizing that my words of encouragement are no different from those of the friendly neighbourhood atheist photographer can sometimes leave us a bit uneasy about the nature of the encouragement we are offering. Is what I'm saying really 'Christian'? If it is, then **how** is it Christian? If it isn't, should I stop? Are there compartments in our speaking, where some of what we say—like direct evangelism—is definitely 'Christian', and other things are just words that anyone might have said, Christian, Buddhist or atheist?

If we do feel like this, it's probably not because we are being too gospel-minded about our conversation. Rather, it's quite possible that we are not being gospel-minded enough. Let me explain.

The world we live in is God's world. He made it—all of it, not just the Christian, 'churchy' bits of it. He made sea slugs, relationships and stars. God created human beings who are smart enough to begin to understand creation, exercise authority over it (as commanded in Genesis 1-2), and in their spare time build cubby houses. He made the world, and us, by his word of wisdom. Here's what Proverbs 8 has to say about the relationship between God's wisdom and the world:

> "The LORD possessed me [wisdom] at the beginning
> of his work,
>   the first of his acts of old.
> Ages ago I was set up,
>   at the first, before the beginning of the earth.
> When there were no depths I was brought forth,
>   when there were no springs abounding with water.
> Before the mountains had been shaped,
>   before the hills, I was brought forth,
> before he had made the earth with its fields,
>   or the first of the dust of the world.

When he established the heavens, I was there;
    when he drew a circle on the face of the deep,
when he made firm the skies above,
    when he established the fountains of the deep,
when he assigned to the sea its limit,
    so that the waters might not transgress his
        command,
when he marked out the foundations of the earth,
    then I was beside him, like a master workman,
and I was daily his delight,
    rejoicing before him always,
rejoicing in his inhabited world
    and delighting in the children of man." (Prov 8:22-31)

God made the world with wisdom, and he made it good. What's more, it's a wisdom that is not hidden from the average citizen. You too can be wise! God's wisdom is communicated to us in words. So in this same chapter of Proverbs, wisdom speaks and says:

"To you, O men, I call,
    and my cry is to the children of man.
O simple ones, learn prudence;
    O fools, learn sense.
Hear, for I will speak noble things,
    and from my lips will come what is right,
for my mouth will utter truth;
    wickedness is an abomination to my lips." (Prov 8:4-7)

The key to getting this wisdom is to "fear the LORD", since "the fear of the LORD is the beginning of wisdom" (Prov 9:10). For us today, to fear the Lord means to acknowledge his Son, Jesus, as Lord, and trust him for the forgiveness of our sin. It follows that through the Lord Jesus, Christians have special access to the wisdom of God in dealing with his creation.

Here's an example for comparison. Imagine you are an experienced mechanic working in a family-owned automobile factory that manufactures the best family station wagon in the world. This station wagon has everything that opens and shuts—an espresso machine, a drop-down digital television with a satellite dish, global positioning system and automatic navigation, wireless internet connection, and vertical-take-off-and-landing capabilities for those tight city parking situations. It's a miracle of space-age technology and family planning.

The point is that you (as the mechanic who works in the factory of the owner-designer, and acknowledges his genius) are also the person best placed to learn how to repair and maintain this brilliant new car.

Now it's true that someone else who does not work for the factory, and who doesn't know the owner-designer from a bar of soap, could have a go at doing exactly the same repairs as someone like you who works for the factory. After all, the local backyard mechanic is not completely ignorant. He or she may well have grown up assembling and disassembling the automotive icons of the early '70s (the Valiant Charger is still a fond memory for many). He or she may have developed their own practical wisdom about how cars generally tend to work, and will certainly be able to have a stab at repairing the vertical-take-off-and-landing capabilities of your station wagon. Why not? As a matter of fact, I have yet to meet the mechanic who admitted that a car problem I presented to them was beyond them. My wallet always seems to be the limiting factor, so they tell me anyway.

Indeed over time, the really gifted backyard mechanic might get quite good at the required repairs to this uber-wagon, to the point where he may even be more skilful than some of the junior apprentices at the factory. But the real, best and latest wisdom on how to build the wagon and keep it going is always going to rest with the owner-designer back at head office.

Now every analogy, like a station wagon's rear tyres, needs adjustment and alignment, and you may feel completely free to add your own little tweaks to this illustration to make it work for you. But the point of the comparison should be clear. The only one who truly understands **creation** is God **the Creator**. He is the owner-designer of the universe and everything in it. Not only does he understand it, but he also keeps it and every single thing in it going from moment to moment, as we reminded ourselves in Chapter 2.

Within God's creation, Christians are people who worship God the Creator through his Son, Jesus Christ. We may not have perfect wisdom about every detail of creation, but we have something better: we are related as children to the one who does, and who gladly shares his knowledge of the world through his word. "We have the mind of Christ", says Paul (1 Cor 2:16).

When we come to speak to others, therefore, about everyday life here in the creation, we are in a superb position to be able to speak a word of wisdom because we know the wise Creator.

A practical example: sex

A practical example may help here. The Bible says that faithfulness in marriage really matters. This is not a hard concept to understand, nor is it difficult to find such teaching in different parts of the Bible, both Old and New Testament. Nor should it surprise us that the Bible might have a reasonable amount to say on the subject, given that God is the creator of men and women and marriage, and that our relationship as men and women is quite fundamental to our right ruling over God's creation (see Gen 1-2).

This teaching of the Bible occurs almost completely without reference to romantic love as the basis for choosing a mate, much less the idea of having sex with multiple partners before deciding which one to get married to (a theory of mate-selection that is now unfortunately common in Western society).

Now, it is not as if the Bible is against romantic and erotic love between a man and a woman (see Jacob's love for Rachel in Genesis 29, or the love between the man and woman in Song of Songs). Nevertheless, the Bible puts romance and erotic love in perspective—namely, that good and lasting relationships are about keeping your marriage promises, not about who you happen to be romantically attracted to within any given six month period.

Consequently, it makes sense, having read and understood the Bible's teaching on the matter, that the **wise** course of action would be to choose a marriage partner not so much according to whether they are sexually or romantically attractive, but on the basis of whether they are faithful to their word. Marriage is about promise-keeping, and if someone is deceitful in small things, it is unlikely that they will be truthful in this most important of human relationships.

This practical wisdom can be extended. Once we are married, it makes sense to keep doing things to strengthen that marriage, rather than looking for romantic fulfilment elsewhere. It may even make sense, in the absence of a potential marriage partner who is able to keep their word, to remain unmarried!

Having said all this, it is perfectly true that this biblical wisdom from the Creator can also be understood (at least in part) without any reference to the gospel. Indeed, hundreds of thousands of secular research dollars have been expended to reach similar conclusions or make related observations, and in the process enhance the postgraduate career and earning capacity of many a cunning boffin. The anthropologist Dr Helen Fisher of Rutgers University has done long-term research into the interaction between neurotransmitters dopamine and norepinephrine, and the interaction of such brain chemicals with feelings of romance and sexual attraction. She advises: "Don't copulate with people you don't want to fall in love with because it may just happen to you."[1] In a

---

[1]   Quoted from an interview with Dr Laura Berman, found at
http://www.newshe.com/wsh2004b/fisher.html. Dr Fisher's
anthropological research into romantic love is documented in books
such as *Why We Love: The Nature and Chemistry of Romantic Love*,
Henry Holt & Co., New York, 2004.

similar vein and after much government-sponsored research, Dorothy Tennov and Cindy Hazan are able to conclude that romantic love is incapable of being sustained much beyond three years.[2] Some secular thinkers are able to take this further, and in a flash of logical and empirically-tested genius, will be able to put these two research factoids together with other bits of information. They will then conclude that for some, promiscuous sex before marriage really is a most complicated matter that quite possibly will not lead to a lasting, healthy, happy relationship with someone of the opposite sex. Such is the power of human reason.

Now in biblical terms, this research is not the stuff of headlines. It simply confirms what we would expect from reading what the Bible says in numerous places, and reflecting on how God has designed men and women for faithful permanent relationships within marriage.

So because the Bible is God's word, and because God is the creator of everything, Christians can speak to others with the wisdom that God gives in his word—not only about the gospel, as fundamental and basic as this is, but about everything in creation.

The having of such wisdom is of course no **guarantee** that our words will be wise in every situation. Of course we will get it wrong—just as the mechanic who trained in

---

[2]   Tennov's work and similar research by Cindy Hazan at Cornell University, reported in 'That crazy little thing called love', *The Observer*, Sunday 14 December 2003 (Hazan's name is misspelled in the article).

the owner-designer's factory will still occasionally, through ignorance or inability or carelessness, manage to throw a spanner in his boss's works. In the same way, our capacity to get things spectacularly wrong as Christians is probably no different from that of any other human being. But because the Bible speaks clearly, we have a gracious, God-given head start in being able to apply God's wisdom to our daily lives. Christians have words of encouragement to say, not just in gospel matters, but in every area of life in which God's wisdom can be brought to bear. This is all a part of speaking the truth in love.[3]

Gospel and wisdom

It's important as we think about this to be clear on one point: none of this wisdom we've just discussed is ultimately separate from the gospel. For one thing, every true piece of wisdom comes from the one God. But as well as this, we should remember that the gospel itself is not some add-on bonus, like a spare memory card for the digital camera, or like five extra jelly dinosaurs to plop on top of a birthday cake.

Rather, the gospel is God's **supreme** wisdom, revealed to those who trust him. If wisdom is a mountain, the gospel stands at its summit and makes sense of the whole. So Paul, in speaking about the cross of Christ, the heart of the gospel, says this:

---

[3]   Again, you may like to refer back to the original definition of Christian encouragement in Chapter 1.

> For Jews demand signs and Greeks seek wisdom, but we preach Christ crucified, a stumbling block to Jews and folly to Gentiles, but to those who are called, both Jews and Greeks, Christ the power of God and the wisdom of God. (1 Cor 1:22-24)

"Christ crucified" is the power and wisdom of God because in his life, death and resurrection, Jesus Christ shows us what God himself is like. Not only does he show us, but because he has died for our sins and offered forgiveness, he has brought us into friendship with God the heavenly Father. The **showing** of God's wisdom in Christ leads to the **knowing** of the one who gives it—that is, God. We need only stop trusting in ourselves, and in our own righteousness and goodness, to receive this wisdom and power from God.

What's more, from the perspective of this gospel of Jesus Christ, all other wisdom in creation can truly be understood. As a result of Jesus' death and resurrection, we see confirmed what the Bible has taught from Genesis 1—that creation has one purpose only. The purpose of creation is to bring glory to God, through our Lord Jesus Christ.

Those who live their lives without God can't see this. For them, creation has neither meaning nor purpose. For them, we struggle on as best we can, dealing with a world going nowhere. For them, wisdom means treating Jesus as largely irrelevant, instead devising their own framework of what is good and true and worthwhile. Yet this wisdom of the world is overturned by the grace of

God. Listen to Paul again:

> But God chose what is foolish in the world to shame
> the wise; God chose what is weak in the world to
> shame the strong; God chose what is low and despised
> in the world, even things that are not, to bring to
> nothing things that are, so that no human being might
> boast in the presence of God. (1 Cor 1:27-29)

The old creation will be done away with on the day of judgement. The new creation will be creation restored to perfection; a place where God rests as he did on the seventh day because everything he has done is "very good". All who trust in Jesus will be a part of this new creation. In this new creation, the Lord Jesus will wipe away every tear from the eyes of his children, "and death shall be no more, neither shall there be mourning nor crying nor pain anymore, for the former things have passed away" (Rev 21:4).

Words of prayer

Once we've seen how God rules all things through his wisdom, especially in the gospel, we are able to see just how important it is to pray. Any Christian who wants to speak words of encouragement and wisdom to others has to start from the position of recognizing God's sovereignty. God rules over every single thing that happens, in order to achieve his own purposes and glory. Our thinking about the world and everything in it will be completely out of kilter if we don't start with this assumption.

If we do realize that God is in control of his world, then the first word relating to someone's encouragement may not be spoken to another person at all. Rather, the one we will speak to is God, who knows exactly and perfectly every single thing about the situation the other person is in, and thus knows precisely what they need. What's more, he is the only one, ultimately, who is able to meet that need. That is why the Bible so often tells us to bring our concerns to God in prayer:

> Humble yourselves, therefore, under the mighty hand of God so that at the proper time he may exalt you, casting all your anxieties on him, because he cares for you. (1 Pet 5:6-7)

> The Lord is at hand; do not be anxious about anything, but in everything by prayer and supplication with thanksgiving let your requests be made known to God. And the peace of God, which surpasses all understanding, will guard your hearts and your minds in Christ Jesus. (Phil 4:5-7)

Once we realize that God is in charge and knows everything, then prayer for others won't be some hurried afterthought. There'll be no sense of apologizing when we say to someone, "All I can do at the moment is pray". Prayer to the God who is supreme over all is the most significant contribution we can make to someone's encouragement.

Not only so, but our very ability to speak to others with wisdom comes from God, and ought to be a subject for prayer:

> If any of you lacks wisdom, let him ask God, who gives generously to all without reproach, and it will be given him. But let him ask in faith, with no doubting, for the one who doubts is like a wave of the sea that is driven and tossed by the wind. For that person must not suppose that he will receive anything from the Lord; he is a double-minded man, unstable in all his ways. (Jas 1:5-8)

If we don't pray for wisdom, we shouldn't expect to receive wisdom. And without God's wisdom, we shouldn't be surprised when something we say that seems terribly wise to us turns out to be quite silly. We may find that we are speaking out of ignorance. We may be demonstrating by our words that we have completely misunderstood a situation, or that we are unable to listen to someone beyond the first sentence of their question. Like Job's three friends in the book of Job, we may know certain truths but through lack of real wisdom gained by prayer, our application of the truth may be foolish, wrong-headed and disastrous. "Like a lame man's legs, which hang useless, is a proverb in the mouth of fools" (Prov 26:7).

As a specific example, I have heard of situations where Christians suffering from treatable medical conditions have been urged by other Christians to give up their medication as a way of showing their faith in God. In some instances, the results of such advice have been disastrous, even fatal, revealing profound ignorance on the part of the advice-giver about both the medical condition and the way God normally intervenes to help those who are sick. Who knows what physical and psychological damage might have been averted if the Christians giving such advice had only stopped and prayed sincerely to God for wisdom as to what to say?

This is an extreme example, but the point is clear. We ought to pray, and pray often, for wisdom. God is a loving and gracious Father, who rules his world and wants to give good things to his children. Again and again, the Bible encourages us to ask for those good things, including wisdom, and expect that he will respond favourably and with great kindness.

Finally, and perhaps most significantly, we should always be praying that God would use our words of encouragement to bring about change in the lives of others. As we noticed in our last chapter, our job is to plant and water, and God's job is give the growth, through the inward work of his Holy Spirit.

We are dependent on God's Spirit for every single thing to do with our encouragement of others. We depend on his Spirit not simply for the words to say, and the wisdom to know when and how to say them; we depend on him even to open the eyes and ears and heart of the other person to receive God's wisdom and be changed by it. This should drive us to prayer. Let us follow the Apostle Paul's example in asking God to change the hearts of our hearers:

> I do not cease to give thanks for you, remembering you in my prayers, that the God of our Lord Jesus Christ, the Father of glory, may give you a spirit of wisdom and of revelation in the knowledge of him,

having the eyes of your hearts enlightened, that you may know what is the hope to which he has called you, what are the riches of his glorious inheritance in the saints, and what is the immeasurable greatness of his power towards us who believe ... (Eph 1:16-19)

Chapter 6

SPEAKING UP

Most of us don't get stage fright as badly as Bilbo Baggins did. Ian Holm, who played Bilbo Baggins in *The Lord of the Rings* movies, had an attack of stage fright in 1976 that led to him walk off stage in the middle of a live performance of *The Iceman Cometh*. So badly was he affected that he didn't feel able to return to live theatre for a full fifteen years.

Actually, most of us don't get stage fright at all, for the very good reason that most of us don't go on stage. We don't have the problem because we never take the risk.

All the same, there is something about **any** situation where we have to speak to others that is, potentially at least, rather scary—even if the stage is our lounge room and our audience is an audience of one. When we speak, we expose something of ourselves and our thoughts to another person. The other person may be accepting of what they see and hear, or they may not. They may even be critical or questioning of us, or upset by what we say.

As a result, offering Christian encouragement—"speaking the truth in love"—can be a nerve-wracking thing to do, especially if we've never thought about how to do it. This is so whether it's the gospel that we're speaking (as we considered in Chapter 4) or some other sort of Christian wisdom (as we considered in Chapter 5). If the speaking is done in front of a group at church, we can feel quite overawed. This anxiety can arise in other places too—perhaps at the office, or in our place of study. So even though we know that "speaking the truth in love" is a great thing to do, we may still lack confidence in our ability to do it well, or feel intimidated by others who seem to do it better. Quick thinkers and articulate speakers can discourage the rest of us from having a go.

So for the faint-hearted in matters of speaking (and that is all of us, at one time or another), let's begin to consider how we can make progress in the matter of Christian speaking. First, we will consider the excellent and useful example of Paul. Then we'll move on to consider what we might say to others, and how we might say it.

The example of Paul

Paul is an excellent example of how "speaking the truth in love" works out in practice.[1] He's an excellent example:

---

[1]   In one sense, Paul's ministry was unique. God gave him a very specific task: that of preaching the gospel to the Gentiles (Acts 9:11-16). Unlike Paul,

(a) because he did it (always helpful in an example); and (b) because he was not particularly good at it! At least, he was no good by the standards of the day. If this seems hard to believe, remember that he himself says he had ...

> ... decided to know nothing among you except Jesus Christ and him crucified. And I was with you in weakness and in fear and much trembling, and my speech and my message were not in plausible words of wisdom, but in demonstration of the Spirit and of power, that your faith might not rest in the wisdom of men but in the power of God. (1 Cor 2:2-5)

So even if Paul had the "in love" bit of "speaking the truth in love" right, his loving attitude by itself wasn't enough to create an impression amongst the professional speakers of the day. It seems he was not what we would call a 'dynamic' speaker.

There's an important lesson here. Being gifted to speak impressively (by human standards) is almost completely irrelevant to Christian speaking—I say 'almost' because a Christian church leader should still be "able to

---

we can't say that our words have been given to us directly from God. But when we read what Paul actually says, we can't help but see how often Paul sets himself up as an example of what it means to be a Christian. "Be imitators of me, as I am of Christ", he says to the Corinthians (1 Cor 11:1), speaking particularly about removing any obstacle to evangelism. To the Thessalonians, he notes with approval how "you became imitators of us and of the Lord" (1 Thess 1:6). Ultimately, it's the example of Jesus' humility in serving others that we are following in our speaking and acting (Phil 2:5-11).

teach" (1 Tim 3:2). And obviously, some of us are better speakers than others. But Paul tells the Corinthians that the gospel is effective not only **in spite** of his weakness, but that it is effective **because** he is so obviously weak. In 2 Corinthians 12:9, God says to Paul regarding his 'thorn in the flesh' that "my grace is sufficient for you, for my power is made perfect in weakness". Paul therefore says that he will "boast all the more gladly of my weaknesses, so that the power of Christ may rest upon me".

Perhaps this was a point that the proud and gifted Corinthians needed to hear, because Paul makes it again in 2 Corinthians 4. In speaking about his glorious ministry of proclaiming Jesus Christ as Lord, he emphasizes that "we have this treasure in jars of clay, to show that the surpassing power belongs to God and not to us" (2 Cor 4:7). Our weakness and lack of polish is never an obstacle to speaking the truth in love—indeed, it is the normal way God works, using frail, sinful people like us as his fellow workers.

Paul is an example to us in other ways too. In this passage from Acts, he gives a summary of ministry amongst the Ephesians:

> Now from Miletus he sent to Ephesus and called the elders of the church to come to him. And when they came to him, he said to them: "You yourselves know how I lived among you the whole time from the first day that I set foot in Asia, serving the Lord with all humility and with tears and with trials that happened to me through the plots of the Jews; how I did not shrink from declaring to you anything that was profitable, and teaching you in public and from house to house,

testifying both to Jews and to Greeks of repentance towards God and of faith in our Lord Jesus Christ." (Acts 20:17-21)

These five verses are very handy for Christians wanting to get a handle on Paul's basic method of operation. It's a snapshot of a three-year period of ministry in one place, and it shows very well how Paul put his principles of speaking God's word into practice. In the course of showing us what he **did** do, we also learn a bit about what he **didn't** do. Paul was not the sort of preacher who appeared to the congregation once a week but for the rest of the time locked himself in his study and kept his distance. He didn't surround himself or the gospel with defences or blockades, making it difficult for people to hear him or his message. He taught God's word "in public and from house to house". He wasn't stuck-up. He wasn't arrogant. He wasn't distant or unapproachable. There was no part of ministry or gospel service that he wouldn't touch.

Paul taught his people humbly "and with tears". What's more, there was no detail of doctrine that Paul felt was too difficult to speak out about, as long as it was profitable to the hearers. Note, "profitable"; not "enjoyable", "entertaining", "easy to hear" or "easy to bear". Some of this teaching may have been hard to understand, as parts of Paul's letters are. But from what we know of Paul's ministry, the real difficulties came when people didn't like certain parts of the message of free grace that they were hearing.

The picture of how Paul conducted his ministry is filled out from other parts of his writing. In Thessalonica and

Corinth, he taught the Bible at his own expense, not charging for it like the professional speakers did. He did everything he could to get the message out: he wrote, preached, spoke, debated, declared and taught the gospel. He did it in large groups and small; he did it with individuals. When he couldn't, he sent friends like Timothy and Titus to make sure the job got done.

Not only this, but he suffered. In 2 Corinthians 11, and in Acts, we hear of Paul's shipwrecks, beatings, imprisonments, persecutions and rejection. In skimming through the story of Paul's life, it is shocking to realize just how often he is forcibly thrown out of one place only to re-surface in a nearby town—preaching the exact same message that got him into trouble in the previous place. He organized for his good friend Timothy to be circumcised as an adult, in order not to place an obstacle in the path of evangelism (Acts 16:3). He was consistently careless of the personal cost of gospel preaching, so long as it happened. We are not aware of any specific limitation on the particular method he used to speak God's word, so long as that word was clearly heard.

Indeed, the only limitation Paul observed in speaking God's word was that he was never dishonest. He never 'spun' his message in a deceitful way, so that people would hear only the bits that appealed to them, and miss out on the difficult bits (see 2 Cor 4:1-2). He gave the full message —both the bad news of judgement and suffering, as well as the wonderful news of God's love and grace. He was transparently honest in his presentation. He didn't flatter people, or change the message to suit them—and nor should we.

We can sum up by saying that Paul used any honest method available to him to help his hearers understand the message of the gospel—as well as see it lived out in his life. Nor did he hesitate to declare any part of not just the gospel but "the whole counsel of God" (Acts 20:27). With Paul's example in mind, let's consider what we say, and how we are to say it.

What we say: case studies and principles

As we've already noted, our speech as Christians will not only be about the gospel but will flow over into every area of life (see Chapter 5 on 'wisdom'). Let's take three examples of how God's word might shape our speaking in particular areas. The three examples are politics, suffering and sex.

Example 1: Politics

In most parts of the Western world, most people have nothing good to say about politicians. Is this a right attitude? The Bible would say 'No', and point out that we should respect and honour our leaders, knowing that God has put them there (e.g. Rom 13:1-7). The Bible also says that our conversation should be "gracious, seasoned with salt" (Col 4:6).

Putting this sort of teaching together with other parts of the Bible, what should a Christian do when the topic of politics comes up in conversation? Should we join the throng, blasting away at the faults of our political leaders? After all, it's a free country, and there's no doubt that leaders often deserve to be criticized, some more than others. What's more, Christians who want to be free to talk about an unpopular idea like the gospel should be fans of free speech. Public criticism of leaders is not only occasionally justified, but is an essential part of protecting our freedom to say other things that people may not want to hear. Just because you criticize someone doesn't mean you're showing disrespect.

On the other hand, much of our criticism of politicians **is** disrespectful. There may be times when our silence amidst the attacks of others will speak volumes. Going beyond this, we might consider how to tie the issue in to the gospel itself. We might talk, for example, about how Jesus restores faith in leadership, because he uses his power not to dominate but to serve those in society who are weak and have no help.

There's no one right answer here. Some moral issues are clear-cut (a judge changing a just ruling in response to a bribe is always wrong—see Deut 16:19), and we should feel free not only to express our view on this, but to explain where we get it from. In other areas we have great freedom, and we should reflect this as we speak. The Bible isn't left-wing and it isn't right-wing. But it turns our thinking about good leadership completely upside down, making it an issue of character and service, not charisma and bossiness.[2]

---

[2]   A good book on the subject of Christian thinking about the world is Harry Blamires, *The Christian Mind: How should a Christian think?*, Vine Books, Michigan, 1997 (1963).

Example 2: Suffering

What we believe as Christians affects every area of life. Consider a second, quite different example: what do we say to the person who is suffering long-term illness, or some related difficulty or grief? Again, the Bible isn't silent—although let's first of all notice that it might encourage **us** to be silent for quite some time! "Weep with those who weep" says Romans 12:15. There is a lot to be said for not jumping in with good advice, especially when someone's suffering is great. True Christian love may mean doing some child-minding and saying nothing, recognizing that there is "a time to keep silence, and a time to speak" (Eccl 3:7). Remember the three friends who went to comfort Job in his trouble? They had a great deal to say, but once we have reached the end of Job's 42 chapters, we could be forgiven for thinking that the most useful and comforting thing they managed to do in the entire book was to sit in silence for a week.[3]

Nevertheless, when it is time to speak (and there almost always will be such a time), the Bible presents some ideas about suffering that no-one except a Christian would hold to. Christians proclaim that God is not a distant God who enjoys seeing us suffer, but a God who sent his only Son to suffer and die in our place, and to rise again to put us right with our heavenly Father. No-one could ever accuse the

---

[3] "And they sat with him on the ground seven days and seven nights, and no one spoke a word to him, for they saw that his suffering was very great" (Job 2:13).

biblical God of being distant and uncaring. What's more, passages such as Hebrews 12:1-13 and Romans 5:1-11 tell us that our suffering has a point to it, and can bring strength, perseverance and the assurance that we are loved by God.[4] If we know and believe these things, then we have a very powerful message of comfort to offer those who suffer—a message that no-one but Christians could know or share.

Again, it is worth remembering that when we seek to encourage those who are suffering, we will most likely not download these Bible references and Bible ideas in one conversation, or expect that once said, the message will be immediately heard, remembered and acted upon. It will take time and perseverance and patience. And we will pray, not only that God would relieve their suffering, but that he would open their hearts to receive his word about their suffering.

Case study 3: Sex

What might we say to the man or woman who is thinking of starting an adulterous relationship? This is an area where Christians will sound less and less like the world around us, as we apply the gospel to our sexual behaviour and relationships. Worldly wisdom and secular counsellors are prone to advise people having serious marriage difficulties to give up—just walk away from a

---

[4]   Readers who want to follow this up will appreciate Don Carson's book, *How Long, O Lord? Reflections on Suffering and Evil*, IVP, Leicester, 1990.

difficult relationship. You will be happier, your partner will be happier, and the person you are attracted to will be happier when you begin to pursue them.

Statistically, such advice is highly dubious. Simply tracing the divorce statistics for first marriages, and noting how they escalate for second, third or fourth marriages, is quite enough to refute the suggestion that we will be happier out of our existing marriages and in new ones. The Bible doesn't bother with statistics, but simply says things like "You shall not commit adultery" (Exod 20:14), and "Let the marriage bed be undefiled, for God will judge the sexually immoral and adulterous" (Heb 13:4).

But having spelt out the basic Christian position on adultery, there is quite a bit more to say. I once had the misfortune to sit through an entire sermon on 1 Corinthians 6. Believe me when I say that the problem was not 1 Corinthians 6. In this excellent chapter of Corinthians, the subject of sexual immorality is covered in some detail and from a number of angles. In the sermon, we were told not to commit adultery. We were reminded that homosexuality was a sin. We were cautioned against visiting prostitutes. Various other exhortations and instructions followed, and for all I know they may have been quite relevant to a number of the hearers.

Not once, however, did the speaker touch on the fundamental reason for this changed behaviour, which is stated quite clearly, smack bang in the middle of the chapter that he was preaching on. 1 Corinthians 6:11 says: "But you were washed, you were sanctified, you were justified in the name of the Lord Jesus Christ and by the Spirit of our God". This is the very heart of the Christian message—that we are saved from sin through the work of the Lord Jesus. By omitting this rather crucial fact, the preacher had managed to preach a sermon that was little more than legalistic moralism, with a few practical tips and behavioural hints thrown in, but no mention whatsoever of the grace of forgiveness available in Jesus, or the reality that change and hope lies with God alone, not our own efforts.

As we speak to people about moral issues (such as adultery), we must not be like the neglectful preacher, and fail to mention the gospel of grace.

In each of these three brief case studies, we have only just begun to consider how trusting God's word, and thinking about its application, will shape our thinking and speaking. Not only is there much more that could be said about each of these areas, but there is no end to the number of different topics on which we might be able to offer a Christian view. The Bible has lots to say about everything. Indeed, you may have seen those Bibles where there is an index not just for key words, but for topics, with Bible verses to look up when you are feeling joyful, happy, sad and (for all I know) if you happen to be planning the first manned space mission to Mars.

In fact as a marketing idea, it has occurred to me that you could sell an entire book including such popular subjects as 'playing the stockmarket', 'putting the spark back in your marriage', 'what to do on a dull Saturday afternoon', 'how to overhaul the evening service at church' and 'keeping your Tamagotchi alive'. Under each topic the relevant passages from the Bible could be placed, with a few pithy comments, and by the end of the process you would have either a phone-book-sized directory or a searchable CD with answers relating to any topic of Christian living and application. In fact, if you had this exhaustive CD, you would hardly need your Bible any more! You could simply type in the words "failed romance", for example, and the CD would deliver all the relevant verses and perhaps some web links to Christian dating sites. Indeed, I have held back from looking too closely at Christian book catalogues recently out of the vague fear that someone has already stolen this concept.

The whole idea is nonsense, of course. The Bible is a book about God, not a book about us. We need to read it not simply to get answers to specific problems but to learn about God as he shows himself to us. Although the Bible speaks about all of life, it doesn't offer a one-size-fits-all solution to every single situation we encounter in life, as if we can simply flip to a verse and get the instant answer. Instead, it teaches us about who God is, and the grace and freedom that come through Jesus Christ. It teaches us about ourselves and about other people. It provides us with a map and a compass to know where we're going, as well as advice about the problems we'll encounter along the way. As we seek to apply this knowledge to the constantly varying and new situations we confront every day, we won't always get it right. This side of glory, we recognize that our knowledge and ability to deal with things is limited. We will still struggle to know what to say or do when a family member gets cancer, or when we face a decision about employment, or when our country decides to support or declare a war.

On some matters we will be quite certain: Jesus died for the sins of the world, and the world needs to hear about it. On other matters, we will see that even though the issue is not as central as the gospel, we still ought to speak clearly as Christians: it is wrong to leave your wife; we ought to oppose abortion; we should look out for the needs of our neighbours. On still other matters, we may feel less certain, but we will still seek to apply the Bible's teaching as best we can: this would be a better job than that because it will allow you to spend more time with your family and make it easier to get to a Bible study; this government policy looks like it will help the unemployed, so we should consider writing to the local member of Parliament and thanking him for it; and so on.

In all of this, we need to begin with "the fear of the LORD", which is the beginning of wisdom. We need to keep reading God's word, where this wisdom will be found. And we need to keep praying to him to grant us that wisdom in the midst of our frailty and uncertainty. We also need to keep talking with each other, and helping each other: "Without counsel plans fail, but with many advisers they succeed" (Prov 15:22).

And as we think and pray and discuss, we shouldn't be afraid to go the next step and **speak**, remembering that Paul was not frightened to declare "the whole counsel of

God". Whatever the question, Christians who love to encourage others in a **Christian** way will be reading their Bibles, thinking through the questions, praying about them, asking advice, and above all, boldly speaking about what they think and why they think it.

This is "speaking the truth in love".

Chapter 7

How we say what we say

Readers may be aware of the soldier whose wife died, and whose drill-sergeant was told to break the news to him as gently as possible.

The sergeant strode over to the barracks and bellowed, "Jones, shine your shoes! Brown, clean the windows! Smith, you're excused from kitchen duty because your wife's died! Wilson, report for guard duty ...".

We've worked out that it's important to speak, but how should we say what we say?

The best advice of all is to follow the command to "love your neighbour as yourself" (Matt 19:19), along with "whatever you wish that others would do to you, do also to them, for this is the Law and the Prophets" (Matt 7:12). We should speak the truth in love. This will not always mean saying comfortable or easy things in a pleasant way—"Faithful are the wounds of a friend;

profuse are the kisses of an enemy" (Prov 27:6). But our overriding concern in how we speak will be the other person's best interest.

With this overarching law of love in mind, let us consider five principles. They are not the final word on the subject by any means, but they are examples of how "speaking the truth in love" might work in practice:

1. Always remember the gospel of grace and repentance
2. Be specific
3. Be humble
4. Deal with important issues
5. There is a time for silence

1. Remember the gospel of grace and repentance

This point is far more important than the rest, so we will spend more time on it.

We are aiming, in our encouragement, to bring people to Christ-likeness. This can only happen in one way: as people hear and respond to the gospel of grace. The first word and last word we speak should be a word of grace. "Let your speech always be gracious", says Paul in Colossians 4:6. Grace, as found in the gospel, is the enemy of legalism, rule-making, and the giving of five helpful tips. Grace means basing what we say in the gospel itself; a gospel which teaches forgiveness, mercy, and a strength for living that comes from God's Holy Spirit and not from ourselves.

Those who have read *The Lord of the Rings* or, even better, seen the three movies (which is more time efficient, though only just) will know that there is only one place in Middle Earth where an evil Ring of Power can be conveniently melted down, and that is in the fires of the crack of Mount Doom in Mordor. (If you didn't already know that, apologies for spoiling the ending, and did you know that the woman in *The Crying Game* is really a man, and that Darth Vader is Luke Skywalker's father?)

But moving on, my point is that there ought to be a very special, uniquely powerful Crack-of-Doom furnace of white hot intensity created specifically for the burning of Christian books containing legalism; the sort of furnace so hot that it incinerates even the people approaching it as they manoeuvre the garbage-bag-loads of legalistic books in their quivering arms. *Seventy-seven Disciplines for Bible Reading.* Fwoosh! *One Hundred and Ten Tips for Praying More Effectively. You Can Do Better. Your Children Can Do Better.* Snap, crackle and flame! *You are a Failure but Buying This Book May Help. Stop Whatever it is You're Doing and Do This Instead.* Let each one of these books, along with every other example of the genre, be obliterated for all eternity. To quote the philosopher David Hume on the burning of books (admittedly completely out of context), "Commit it then to the flames, for it contains nothing but sophistry and illusion".

If I can disclose a personal interest here, legalism makes me feel deeply ill. Whether it's the finger-wagging preacher telling me not to visit prostitutes but neglecting to tell me about the grace and forgiveness available in Jesus; or whether it's the smarmy and overly melodious voice of the lady on the religion programme trying to sell me on the latest package of spiritual disciplines and ways of doing meditation—it makes no difference, they are all bad. Give us a break, preacher-person or radio-lady. If you haven't told us about God who is rich in mercy—worse, if you have and then buried it under a junkyard of legalism—then kindly put a sock in it while I slip away and read my Bible without outside interference. Giving rules without grace is a sickening, dead moralism which has no place in the speech of anyone who wants to encourage people with the word of God.

Having got that off my chest, let's continue. This principle of grace, and starting and ending with it, may still seem a bit too obvious and a bit too abstract. If so, consider this specific example of why we shouldn't steal.

Someone who is simply offering morality and legalism will simply tell people not to steal. In fact, I heard a sermon once on the command "you shall not steal" which said basically this, together with some entertaining but stern morality tales of young shoplifters who came to sticky ends, thrown in from the preacher's days as a supermarket manager. It made me feel that he would have been a good supermarket manager who perhaps could have served the gospel of grace better by remaining where he was.

Now speaking to someone about shoplifting as a Christian would certainly not mean glossing over the fact that stealing is sin. The gospel, after all, includes the message that we are under the judgement of God because we've fallen short of his glory and broken his law. Because stealing is wrong, and because God will judge sin, we should repent.

But to apply the **Christian** wisdom of grace to the situation of the shoplifter would involve, for example, finding out whether the person is stealing out of desperation, perhaps because Christians have been overlooking their responsibility to the poor. "People do not despise a thief if he steals to satisfy his appetite when he is hungry", says the writer of Proverbs (Prov 6:30, although the next verse warns that theft will be punished!).

Even more, it would be gracious to tell the thief about the gospel of grace—about Jesus, who was crucified on the cross next to a thief, and who won forgiveness for thieves and drunkards and liars and all the rest of us. The thief who understands this will stop stealing, because they understand that not only is it wrong, but that it is inconsistent with the generosity (i.e. grace) they've been shown. Paul makes this logical step in Ephesians 4. Because we have become new creations in Christ, therefore "let the thief no longer steal, but rather let him labour, doing honest work with his own hands, so that he may have something to share with anyone in need" (Eph 4:28). The gospel of repentance and grace not only teaches a thief to stop stealing, but it also makes him generous and ready to use his skills to supply the needs of others.

In the same way, Christian encouragement can never be simply the dispensing of rules and advice. We are to return again and again to the gospel of grace, and allow it to shape our response to the person we're speaking to.

2. Be specific

God is the boss of this world. That means that no part of his world, or our place in it, is beneath concern or comment. Exactly how detailed is God's concern for us? In Matthew's Gospel, Jesus says, "Are not two sparrows sold for a penny? And not one of them will fall to the ground apart from your Father. But even the hairs of your head are all numbered. Fear not, therefore; you are of more value than many sparrows" (Matt 10:29-31). That is, God's concern for us goes down to the tiniest detail of our lives.

If God is concerned about detail, we should be too. The Book of Proverbs is full of practical examples of how such concern for the details of life can be observed and applied.

We find proverbs that encourage us simply to notice things, to be observant, and to learn: "Go to the ant, O sluggard; consider her ways and be wise" (Prov 6:6). We can learn from watching the created order; we can learn also from watching people interact: "A gift in secret averts anger, and a concealed bribe, strong wrath" (Prov 21:14).

Other proverbs show quite a nice line in sarcastic humour: "The sluggard buries his hand in the dish and will not even bring it back to his mouth" (Prov 19:24); "It is better to live in a corner of the housetop than in a house shared with a quarrelsome wife" (Prov 21:9).

Now, there are many ways of thinking about and applying these proverbs, but at heart we are being encouraged to reflect on the detail of the world we live in, and to integrate it with what we know of God.

This applies to speaking words of encouragement. It means that we will notice and pay attention to the detail of people's lives. What work do they do? Do they love it or hate it? How would they like to spend their lives? What websites do they visit on the internet? Who inspires them? What did they do on the weekend? Are they in love? Every last bit of someone's life matters to God, which means that like God, we shouldn't write off detail as unimportant.

One caution: this is not the same as being nosey. We don't have the right to know everything about someone's life. As always, the great principle is: "You shall love your neighbour as yourself".

Here's an example of how **not** to do it:

Me: How was your week?

You: Flat out like a lizard drinking, and then some. Pretty upsetting towards the end, too.

Me: I know exactly what you mean. On Monday I woke up late, and had to run for the bus. I got into work and the boss says to me, "So, where's the report?", which is pretty rich, because I was waiting for him to get Fred to send through the figures, and then he said ...

You gave a strong hint that you might want to talk about what happened towards the end of the week. What was it? I missed it because I was too busy talking about me.

Let's say that I did pick up on your hint. Here's how I might have taken the conversation in an encouraging direction:

Me: So what happened?

You: My aunt passed away suddenly. I was very close to her.

Me: That must have been awful. I'm sorry to hear that.

You: Now the fighting begins.

Me: What do you mean?

You: She wasn't married, she's left a unit near the beach, and she has some things from my grandmother there that my mother always thought belonged to her.

A question at the right time, based specifically on what the person said, means that I can listen carefully to what is said next. I can follow up on things that are of genuine concern for the person I'm talking to, without being intrusive.

3. Be humble

Ultimately only God knows where wisdom is to be found. We may be very good at weighing up a situation and giving what we think is the right advice. We may pay careful attention to what we are being told. We may have great insight into the mind of God through his word. But as Proverbs says, "Many are the plans in the mind of a man, but it is the purpose of the LORD that will stand" (Prov 19:21).

Because we don't know everything, we should be humble both in what we say, and how we say it. In human relationships, as in most things, our ignorance is compensated for only by our lack of knowledge. So we may see the person losing their temper, but not see why it happened. And because we know that we don't know everything, it will affect what we say to the person about anger, and possibly whether we say anything at all. Prayer and listening, in the absence of knowing everything, are just as important as speaking boldly when we need to. "Whoever restrains his words has knowledge, and he who has a cool spirit is a man of understanding" (Prov 17:27).

Again, here's an example of me getting it spectacularly wrong:

Me: How did Bible study group go last night, do you think?

You: I found the whole thing a real struggle to be honest.

Me: It was a bit hard, wasn't it? Still, we need to keep at it, don't we? "Let us not neglect to meet together, as some are in the habit of doing", as Hebrews puts it. I tend to find preparing ahead and answering the questions does wonders for my appreciation. Have you tried doing that?

You: Oh, not much recently ...

Me: Did you pray for understanding before the group started? That's also very helpful. Reading a commentary is valuable as well. Which reminds me, did you ever listen to that DVD I lent you—*Adding Pazang to your Bible Gang*? Had some great songs for helping the group to come alive, didn't it? *"Shine, Jesus, shine, fill the earth with ..."*

You: Actually my wife just moved out.

I confess that *Adding Pazang to your Bible Gang* is not at this stage available from Matthias Media, or, truth be known, any reputable Christian organization. However, the rest of the advice could quite easily be found either in the Bible or from wise common sense. The only trouble is, because I've spoken without listening—a good sign of lacking humility—I have given you good cause to be angry at my insensitivity. Humility may affect what I say; it will certainly affect how and when I say it. Sometimes, it will mean that I say nothing at all.

4. Deal with important issues

Just as nothing is too small or trivial for God, nothing is too big for him either. Because God controls all of creation, there is every reason not to get caught up with the small details that everyone else in the world considers to be matters of life and death—you know, what we will eat, drink or wear, possibly where we will live. Jesus said: "Seek first the kingdom of God and his righteousness, and all these things will be added to you" (Matt 6:33).

In practice, this is going to mean bringing the perspective of God's kingdom to bear on all the things **we** think really matter, or that are taking up our time and attention. Now this may indeed, from time to time, mean dealing with small things. Just because some detail of life is small in an eternal perspective is not to say that it lacks importance to the one who is concerned about it at that time. Thus we will want to talk to homeowners and renters about mortgages, we will want to talk to parents about education, and we will want to talk to teenagers and people in their twenties about careers and planning the future. These are things that people consider important.

But because we are dealing with such things from an eternal perspective, and because we want to deal with things that are **genuinely** important in the light of God's kingdom, our answers may occasionally not be the ones expected. If God's kingdom is what really matters, is it the wisest thing to live in such a large house, in such an expensive suburb, requiring such long hours of work? "Whoever gives an honest answer kisses the lips" (Prov 24:26). So we will talk about what matters, in a truthful way, even if that perspective is not always welcome.

The sharp-witted reader will be able to pick up that one of the following examples is how **not** to do this, and the other one might be useful for taking things further.

Example one

You: My wife has just moved out.

Me: Mate, that's awful. Oh, excuse me, I've just seen someone I've been trying to phone all week.

Example two

You: My wife has just moved out.

Me: That's awful.

You: I don't know if she's coming back, and I don't know what I'm going to do.

Me: Do you want to talk about it?

You: I don't know. I just don't know what to do. I'm in shock.

Me: Maybe I can give you a call this afternoon—this is probably not the best place to talk privately. But if there's anything I can do before then, make sure you let me know. Do you need someone to come round now and help with the kids?

You: No, that's OK. I'll talk to you later.

5. There is a time for silence

Ecclesiastes 3:7 says, among other things, that there is a time for everything, "a time to keep silence, and a time to speak". Why should we sometimes be silent? There are at least two reasons.

One vital reason for silence is to allow us to **listen**. This is an important aspect of encouragement, particularly when there is sadness or suffering involved. Listening is both a skill and an attitude. During my counselling training in psychology I received quite a lot of good advice, and some bad advice too, on the **skill** of conveying to others that I was listening to them. This included helpful pointers such as maintaining good eye contact, facing the person, not interrupting, leaning slightly forward (NB. only if sitting!), and reflecting back through various verbal and non-verbal cues that I understood and sympathized with the speaker. I was helped to see that paraphrasing another's words—putting what had been said in a different way—could be an extremely helpful thing to do. Many books of such advice exist, and some go into great detail about specific skills that can be employed.

Some of these ideas are very wise and we would do well to apply them and seek occasional feedback on how well we are doing. I am occasionally reminded by my wife that looking at her when she is speaking ought to be more than a clever theory, half-remembered from university days. Or you may have had the experience of speaking to someone at church or in another group where it's a bit too obvious that they are looking over your shoulder to see if there is someone else that they could speak to. This is an easy trap to fall into when you are wanting to be welcoming to newcomers.

However, it is very important to distinguish between the **skill** of showing that we are listening, and the **reality** of attending to someone's words. Skills may be learnt, mimicked and even pretended. At the heart of true listening is not a set of skills but **other-person-centred-ness**—a love and respect for the person speaking to us that puts their interests before our own, and is reflected in the way we use our ears and our body. We are to treat them, in our listening and speaking, in the way we ourselves would like to be treated—indeed, in the way God treats us. God speaks to us with words of truth, grace, and comfort. In his infinite grace, he is delighted to listen to anything that his children would like to say to him. We should have the same attitude.

There is a second reason for keeping silent. Sometimes, we need to have the humility to recognize that we don't know what to say. We may not be ready to speak—we may need time to read God's word and think and pray and talk to others—or we may simply be out of our depth and unable to grasp what words would be encouraging. Proverbs 10:19 is relevant here: "When words are many, transgression is not lacking, but whoever restrains his lips is prudent".

An example of how all this is done well would be hard to put into print! But some of the previous examples in this chapter have shown how it can be done badly. It may be helpful to ask ourselves from time to time what it is that makes us speak when silence would be the better option. Have we pre-judged what the problem is? Do we feel uneasy with silences in a conversation? Being aware of this might help us to do better in talking to people with sensitivity and respect.

OVER THE LAST COUPLE OF CHAPTERS, we've been talking about what to say and how to say it. Let me conclude with one final observation: encouragers don't wait to be asked. There is no requirement whatsoever that before we can begin to speak words of encouragement, we must first be given an official title, role or job description by the church or Christian group of which we are a part. No-one ought to be sitting at home waiting for a written invitation from the pastor to arrive in the mail.

In other words, have a go! Even a simple note of encouragement to a minister or a missionary is worth writing, and all the more valuable for not having been solicited in any way. I know a man who was moved to tears by a simple yet unlooked-for word of thanks from another Christian leader, recognizing that man's years of perseverance in a lonely and difficult mission field. A small word of encouragement like that, spoken at the right time, can be worth more to the one encouraged than a $10,000 contribution to their mission agency. "A word fitly spoken is like apples of gold in a setting of silver" (Prov 25:11).

Chapter 8

IS GOD'S WORD CHANGING *YOU*?

PERHAPS A PSYCHOTHERAPIST could explain why this poem, which I memorized in high school, struck such a chord in my teenage mind:

A man of words and not of deeds
Is like a garden full of weeds
And when the weeds begin to grow
It's like a garden full of snow
And when the snow begins to fall
It's like a bird upon the wall
And when the bird away does fly
It's like an eagle in the sky
And when the sky begins to roar
It's like a lion at the door
And when the door begins to crack
It's like a stick across your back
And when your back begins to smart

It's like a penknife in your heart
And when your heart begins to bleed
You're dead, and dead, and dead indeed.[1]

Possibly one of the things that appealed about this rhyme is that even though there is absolutely no logical connection between one line and the next, there is this ominous 'rightness' about the imagery of the man of empty words succumbing, at last, to a terrible penknife-induced end. The weeds in the garden, the bird of prey high above, the lion terrifyingly near and threatening—every last bit of it speaks of a harsh fittingness about the punishment being meted out upon the unsuspecting fellow full of hollow words. It is the Russell Crowe of nursery rhymes—tough, uncompromising, slightly out of control, but fair at some deep level of the gut.

In this chapter, we consider a number of the reasons why we should take particular care to see that our words and our lives match up. In the course of doing this, we'll consider the role that our actions play in encouraging others.

Reasons for matching actions and words
It is the right thing to do
The first and most important reason that words and actions should match is obvious, but still worth saying: it is just the right thing to do. We know it is right. God expects it of us.

---

[1]   A traditional nursery rhyme.

God himself is like this. What God says reflects who he is; what he promises, he does. It is a characteristic of his that he wants us to emulate: "These are the things that you shall do: Speak the truth to one another; render in your gates judgements that are true and make for peace; do not devise evil in your hearts against one another, and love no false oath, for all these things I hate, declares the LORD" (Zech 8:16-17).

There is a deep and just sense of moral outrage about people who habitually tell lies, whether they are politicians, priests or pizza delivery boys. We know in our heart that lies are wrong. It doesn't need explaining—we simply know that people should do what they say they will. The Bible is scathing about people who profess gospel ethics while failing to live gospel lives. James says: "Religion that is pure and undefiled before God, the Father, is this: to visit orphans and widows in their affliction, and to keep oneself unstained from the world" (Jas 1:27). God makes this complaint, through Isaiah, about Israel's religion:

"When you come to appear before me,
    who has required of you
    this trampling of my courts?
Bring no more vain offerings;
    incense is an abomination to me.
New moon and Sabbath and the calling of
        convocations—
    I cannot endure iniquity and solemn assembly.
Your new moons and your appointed feasts
    my soul hates;
they have become a burden to me;

I am weary of bearing them.
When you spread out your hands,
    I will hide my eyes from you;
even though you make many prayers,
    I will not listen;
    your hands are full of blood.
Wash yourselves; make yourselves clean;
    remove the evil of your deeds from before my eyes;
cease to do evil,
    learn to do good;
seek justice,
    correct oppression;
bring justice to the fatherless,
    plead the widow's cause." (Isaiah 1:12-17)

It is important for the progress of the gospel

The second reason for insisting that gospel actions and gospel words should go together is for the sake of the progress of the gospel itself.

Some years ago, I spoke to a man who explained how his wife's (openly Christian) employer had unilaterally changed an existing agreed job description to give the woman new responsibilities which, if unmet, would result in her receiving a reduced rate of pay. She and her co-workers had learned of the change when they had gone to withdraw money from their bank accounts and discovered that their monthly pay was significantly lower than they'd expected. Upon being confronted, the employer denied any wrongdoing and said that she had already informed the staff team of the changes. If they had misunderstood, the problem was theirs. After a period of considerable financial difficulty for the workers, the registering of formal complaints, further unfulfilled promises and the passing of several months, the matter was eventually put right, but not before a range of questions had been raised about the gap between gospel ethics and actual behaviour of the Christian employer. The employer apologized for any misunderstanding, but in so doing also made it clear that she thought the workers were to blame both for the misunderstanding and, consequently, for most of the difficulty that resulted. Needless to say, the impact for the witness of the gospel was catastrophic.

The Bible makes this point about how the gospel can fall into disrepute because of the failings of those who represent it. You could almost say that the consistent failure of God's people was the reason that there had to be a New Testament! The intention of God in the Old Testament was to bring blessing to the world through Israel. But because of Israel's continual disobedience, Paul could comment (using Isaiah 52:5 as a basis): "as it is written, 'The name of God is blasphemed among the Gentiles because of you'" (Rom 2:24). Israel's repeated disobedience meant that God was dishonoured. As with Old Testament believers, so with Christians.

The other side of this coin is that when our actions **do** back up our words, the impact for the gospel can be massive. Peter says, "Keep your conduct among the Gentiles honourable, so that when they speak against you as evildoers, they may see your good deeds and glorify God on the day of visitation" (1 Pet 2:12). Paul tells Titus that the good works of slaves "adorn the doctrine of God our Saviour" (Tit 2:10). Paul's instructions to Timothy are to "Keep a close watch on yourself and on the teaching. Persist in this, for by so doing you will save both yourself and your hearers" (1 Tim 4:16). When you think about it, this is an amazing thing to say. The way Timothy lives his life in front of those he is teaching will have an impact not only on himself (obviously), but also on those who hear him, for their salvation.

Now, this is not to say that we are saved by anything other than God's grace in the gospel of Jesus. Simply living good lives in front of others will not save them from judgement—indeed the verse just quoted from 1 Peter leaves open the possibility that God will be glorified by his enemies only on the "day of visitation", when they are forced to acknowledge that those who trust Jesus have lived good lives. Nor is people's salvation dependent on us being perfect in behaviour—we will fail, and on occasion the public confession of failure and the associated repentance will be just what people need to see. We are to be people who confess our sin and look for forgiveness, rather than pretending to be perfect. Imagine if the Christian employer who had failed to keep her agreement had gone to her staff and confessed that as a Christian, she realized that she had done wrong and needed to ask forgiveness. Rather than being damaging for the gospel, this would have been a great victory.

There are hundreds of ways in which our good actions will add weight to our words. The friend who actually makes the effort to drop off some food when we are sick makes a far bigger impression than the ten people who said kind words but did nothing further to help.

The minister of one church I attended was a ferocious evangelist. When travelling on the bus, he loved nothing better than to sit next to little old ladies who looked a bit lonely and talk to them about the gospel. He had been known to do this even when they were the only other person on the bus apart from the driver. I suspect it was only his transparent and obvious integrity that meant the police weren't called.

But quite apart from this, he was also known as the most extraordinary doer of good works, often at huge inconvenience to himself. On one occasion a man (let's call him Dave) and his wife began to come to church after he had been attacked in his own home by another man wielding a machete. The attack was related to the sale of drugs.

The reason that Dave started to come to church was that the minister himself had heard about this attack. He had immediately offered personal and practical support. Part of this support involved organizing for a woman he knew—a missionary surgeon on furlough— to perform a unique type of surgery that no other medical expert in the city had been prepared to undertake. This surgery gave Dave back the use of his foot.

The minister had done all of this without any thought of reward for himself or for the church. Needless to say, Dave was a very grateful man. He became willing to hear and listen to the gospel, despite having had nothing to do with the church up until that point.

There was nothing in the minister's action to suggest that his good works were a covert way of getting a gospel opportunity. He had done a good thing simply because it was a good thing, and he'd had the opportunity to do so. Indeed, it is highly likely that his lack of ulterior motive made the gospel that much more attractive.

In the same way we should do good simply because we know that we ought to love our neighbour, and for no other reason. Nonetheless, when we do good, the Bible assures us that the impact for the gospel will be powerful.

Living out the gospel affects our eternal destiny

The final reason for seeing that our words match our actions is given by Paul: "I discipline my body and keep it under control, lest after preaching to others I myself should be disqualified" (1 Cor 9:27). Here Paul raises the terrifying possibility that someone might speak the words of the gospel to others—that we are forgiven only through Jesus, that through his death and resurrection he is now Lord—yet at same time fail to believe it or act on it. "Even the demons believe—and shudder!", says James (Jas 2:19). There are numerous similar warnings in the New Testament about living out what we believe and not turning back to the things we were saved from.

These warnings shouldn't paralyse us with fear. After all, God is faithful and our salvation depends on his action, not on ours. But they serve as a guard against ever becoming complacent, and assuming that just because we know the truth, it follows that we are doing what that truth requires. Unlike the master builder who cuts corners on his own house, or the chef who never eats healthy food, or the gardener whose backyard is full of weeds, we are to put our beliefs into practice.

Do actions speak louder than words?

"Actions speak louder than words." Appealing and intuitively right as this idea sounds, it is fundamentally unchristian. More often than not, it expresses a cynicism about the value of words that should not characterize anyone who believes that God is a speaker, or that Christians have been given the privilege of speaking God's truth to others.

The normal situation, of course, is that we should **both speak and act**. "If a brother or sister is poorly clothed and lacking in daily food, and one of you says to them, 'Go in peace, be warmed and filled', without giving them the things needed for the body, what good is that? So also faith by itself, if it does not have works, is dead" (Jas 2:15-17). Or again: "But if anyone has the world's goods and sees his brother in need, yet closes his heart against him, how does God's love abide in him?" (1 John 3:17). Implied answer: it doesn't.

Nevertheless, there are situations where our nonverbal actions should be allowed to do the talking for us. If a person is in grief, trauma, depression, or experiencing some other suffering, it will occasionally be far better to say nothing, and simply be with them or help them in particular practical ways. "Whoever sings songs to a heavy heart is like one who takes off a garment on a cold day, and like vinegar on soda", says the writer of Proverbs (Prov 25:20). We even find that in some circumstances—such as the case of the believing wife with an unbelieving husband in 1 Peter 3—our silent godly actions may be the very thing God uses to win over someone who knows the gospel but has been resisting it.

Let's not try to drive a wedge between actions and words, or use actions as a substitute for words. Both are important. It is virtually certain that there will come a time in the course of any relationship when it is time to speak. And when that happens, the quality of our actions up to that point will no doubt have a significant effect on how our words are received.

Words matter, but they shouldn't stand alone. We ought to be people who speak the truth in love; we ought to be people who respond to that same truth by serving others with the whole of our lives. Jesus showed us the way: he spoke the truth, called on people to be his followers, and then he died on the cross for the sake of those he revealed God to. As his word and Spirit work in us, so we too speak in love to others, and by our lives "adorn the doctrine of God our Saviour".

Chapter 9

Making a start

If you've become convinced that God's word is indeed powerful to change you and others, and that you have a role in speaking that word, you will want to take the next step. That means either getting started or working out ways to keep going. This chapter opens up some possibilities.

Sitting in church: passenger or driver?

Too many people assume that because church seating is often laid out like a bus, with passengers in the main part and the driver at the front, they should act with appropriate bus-style behaviour. So they board the bus (sit in the pew) at the beginning of the ride, and sit passively while politely following any instructions that the driver issues and trying not to stare or make eye contact with other passengers. When they have reached the desired destination they thank the driver and step off, without at any stage speaking to another passenger.

Some would even see such conversations as an unwelcome intrusion on a quiet and pleasant journey.

But, perhaps surprisingly for some, there is no verse in the Bible that prohibits friendly interaction between people sitting in church pews. Indeed, there are plenty of places in the New Testament where we are urged to see our time together as of the utmost importance in speaking God's word to each other. Those who want to regard church as a private and preferably anonymous experience would do well to read and be corrected by passages such as Hebrews 10:19-25 or 1 Corinthians 12-14 or 1 Peter 4:8-11 or Ephesians 4:1-16 or Romans 12:3-21. In these passages we learn that our personal interaction with other Christians, inside church and outside it, matter a great deal. What we say and do can make a massive difference. If you don't need to be persuaded, read on!

If it is true that words make a difference—and that has been the thrust of this book—we should consider how our words in church could help those around us. Why not consider, for example, coming to church early to speak to others who come early, or to work out where best to sit to meet newcomers? Even speaking a friendly hello to the person who sits in the next seat would be a wonderful start. If that person is your husband or wife or a close friend, you might together consider finding another person, not known to you, and making the effort to be interested in them. Why not pay attention to the sermon, remember a key point, and ask someone after the meeting what they thought of that point?

Perhaps there will be a newcomer at church. Even the

smallest churches have visitors, usually more than you realize until you start to look out for them. One year, I had the enjoyable and worthwhile experience of travelling to many different churches from various denominations while working with the evangelist John Chapman. My job description while with him was to learn to speak by watching him speak. I tried to dress reasonably well, brush my teeth, shave without cutting myself and look more than usually friendly. I don't smoke and it's not a habit of mine to turn up at churches smelling of alcohol (although come to think of it, following the example of Jesus in the Gospels, such a person ought to be made to feel doubly welcome in our meetings). At the end of meetings, I normally loitered with intent (to be friendly) near the tea and coffee table or the church bookstall.

It was surprising and a little disappointing to discover how often I, as an unannounced stranger at a guest service, would be left standing by myself while the regulars spoke to each other or left to go home. I don't mind initiating conversations and so I did. But not all newcomers will be willing to make such an effort, and if we are following the example of Christ, we ought not to expect them to do so.

On other occasions, when I was new at a church I would be greeted and made to feel very much a part of things. At one church where, unknown to most of the congregation, I was soon to be an assistant minister, one of the regulars took it upon himself to tell me how he had been a consistent churchgoer for many years. He had finally realized that good works such as church attendance would not win God's approval. At the same time, he had seen that it was only by trusting Jesus and his death that we could go to heaven. It slowly dawned on me that I was being evangelized. On discovering that I was soon to be employed by the church, this man kept going, and redoubled his efforts to make sure that he told me the gospel. We talked about what it meant that Jesus had died for our sins, and how wonderful it was that we could be forgiven and be completely right with God. Maybe he felt that if his donations to the church were going to be supporting me in ministry, it would be really good if I had a firm grasp on the stuff I was supposed to be teaching him. Anyway, good on him.

It is sometimes very hard to overcome shyness, and not all of us should expect to be good at speaking to strangers. But visitors to church are usually shy themselves, and often feel quite out of place. If it is obvious that your own approach is not smooth, slick and salesmanlike, your own shyness can result in the person feeling even more welcomed than if you were a garrulous, smiling extrovert. They will see that you are sincere. (Naturally the extroverts will want to do their bit too!)

There are many other ways to experience church as one of the many drivers, rather than as a passenger. There is no embarrassment in being part of a large church and introducing yourself to someone who has been there for years. If you joined a sizeable congregation of, say, 200 members, and spoke to two different 'regulars' each week for a year, by the end of the year you would certainly be feeling more comfortable as a part of that church than you did at the beginning. And you would've made new friends with half the congregation. All this encouragement can take place before there is even a hint of having been asked formally to perform some role within the church. You can be a minister of the gospel, and you don't need a written invitation before you can begin. Start now!

Meeting one-to-one

Anyone who has joined a new group or church has had the experience of feeling overwhelmed and, just occasionally, discovering that the group is not as vibrant, friendly or effective as might have been hoped. Still, if it's a group where the Bible is opened and taught, and people are trying to respond by trust and obedience, there is huge potential to do some good.

One obvious place to start is to meet with somebody outside the group and get to know them a bit better. You don't have to have them round for a five-course banquet. It doesn't have to be a big deal. To my astonishment, I've had great conversations with people from my church on the basis of nothing much more substantial than a glass of water. If they want to throw in a double-choc Tim Tam (an Australian biscuit icon not irreparably damaged by the fact that the manufacturing company is now owned by Americans) or maybe a couple of jelly dinosaurs, my joy is complete. If we can't meet in a house, I have been known to sit in a park with a person, at no cost and without being moved on, for more than an hour. This is even cheaper than phoning or emailing.

For some, however, the problem is not money, once the tricky-to-get-time-to-conveniently-get-together factor is solved, perhaps by phone (I recently discovered that I can talk to my sister in Sweden for less than 60¢ an hour). The more pressing question becomes, "What do I say after 'hello'?"

Some gifted blabberers don't find this as much of a problem as me. But even those who are good at talking might like to consider that it is often good to talk about things that are worthwhile. Why not read a psalm and pray through some of the things that are in it? Indeed, you could pick any bit of the Bible, maybe a chapter or half a chapter, and use it as the basis for prayer.[1] Even if we take Peter's point and acknowledge that we may stumble across a few bits in Paul's letters "that are hard to understand" (2 Pet 3:16), the idea is not that we attain perfect and immediate comprehension of everything we are reading. That's what Bible study groups are for. It's enough to understand or be struck by one or two points, which you can then share with the other person and pray about. Of course, reading the Bible and praying is not compulsory for your times of meeting. But given how much blessing is involved in hearing God speak

---

[1]   In the companion course to this book, *Six Steps to Encouragement*, those doing the course meet one-to-one outside the group, read a small part of Ephesians and pray together. This happens five times during the course of the group. Some groups have used this with husbands and wives, and thus seen the additional benefit of starting or promoting the idea of prayer and Bible reading within couples and families.

and asking him to look after us, it would be surprising if we didn't grab hold of this blessing regularly and often.[2]

None of this is difficult to do. Even if you consider yourself to be of limited ability, a regular one-to-one ministry of Bible reading and prayer can do enormous good for the kingdom of God.

My church is too big

I am always faintly surprised when I hear people say, "The trouble is, my church is too big. There are lots of people working away and there's nothing I can contribute." Yet if we have really understood what 'encouragement' means, we should see that the larger and more active the church is, the **more** there is to contribute. Every single Christian needs encouragement, from the senior minister who feels burnt out and disappointed at lack of progress, to the volunteer cleaner who uncomplainingly fixes the church building up on Monday morning after a solid weekend of use, and before the funeral that afternoon. Having more people simply means that there is a greater need for encouragement. This is before we even begin to think about the fact that numbers tend to attract numbers, and that large churches therefore tend to have a much larger

---

[2]   If you're stuck for what to read, or would like something to kick-start your conversation, try using *The Daily Reading Bible* series, or Simon Manchester's little one-to-one booklet *Short Steps for Long Gains*, both published by Matthias Media.

group of people who are nominal in their commitment, or are possibly not even Christian.

There are large churches where the teaching is excellent and the ministry is growing, but where the church struggles to find sufficient small group leaders, or where there are people with short- or long-term difficulties who are easily overlooked. Some see this as simply another cause for complaint, but if you have read this book and understand that every single Christian has a word of encouragement to offer, then you will not be sitting waiting to receive the senior minister's permission slip before you start. Get cracking! Be the person who notices that one of the regulars hasn't shown up at church, and give them a call to see if they are okay. It is enormously encouraging to receive a phone call from someone at church who hasn't been paid to make sure that you are okay, but just happened to notice your absence. Most of us are tempted to complain that we've been overlooked. But we can turn the tables by starting to look out for others.

Still, there are more ways than one to skin the encouragement cat. If your large church has got its act together, it will be looking for ways to grow the gospel by planting or supporting other churches. Help them out. Join one of those new or smaller churches and you will quickly become aware of the possibilities that exist for every single member of the church to do gospel encouragement—possibilities that were there at the large church too, by the way, but may have gotten overlooked in all the activity.

Think of the family

One of the most important ways to encourage each other with God's word is in the family. Husbands are to love and serve wives. Parents are to love and serve children. Brothers and sisters are to care for each other. There are no limits to the care we should be prepared to give: "If anyone does not provide for his relatives, and especially for members of his household, he has denied the faith and is worse than an unbeliever" (1 Tim 5:8). One of the greatest ways of caring for our own family is by sharing God's word together, and praying together, so that God's word is continually shaping the way we relate to each other.

This is particularly a responsibility for fathers. Remember that in the Old Testament—and the theme is continued into the New Testament—the greatest weight for teaching God's commandments rests on the father, or on the father and mother. Professional teachers may help, but it is the job of the Old Testament father to explain to his children the great story of the Passover lamb each year (see Exod 12). And in Proverbs, it's the responsibility of both mother and father to teach wisdom, with children having a corresponding responsibility to listen well, apply this teaching and obey it.[3]

All of us—single, married without children, or parents

---

[3] Tony Payne's book *Fatherhood* (Sydney, Matthias Media, 2005) has some excellent material to help you take these ideas further. The *Table Talk* series and *Short Steps for Long Gains: Family Edition* are also useful resources for family Bible reading (see www.matthiasmedia.com.au for details).

with children—should give careful consideration to how we are using God's word in the relationships we have with those closest to us. If you're single, you may be able to meet with a brother or sister to pray. Or you could have a go at meeting with housemates, or just anybody that you have regular contact with. In the same way as Paul thought of Timothy as his son in the faith (1 Tim 1:2; 2 Tim 1:2), so our spiritual children don't necessarily have to be related by blood. Family responsibility applies within the family of Christ as well.

Grief, trauma, depression and suffering

No-one can go through life without suffering and sadness, and no Christian is exempt from the normal human experiences of difficulty in life. Some problems may be so severe that those going through them feel the need for professional counselling or other medical involvement. Even less severe situations may benefit from the input of outside professionals and helpers.

Nevertheless, the Christian has resources at his or her disposal that no other human being, professional or other-wise, has access too. They have experienced the gospel of grace, and they are able to offer this grace to those around, including those who are suffering. Don't be fooled into thinking that Christian encouragement focuses only on healthy, gifted people whose lives are relatively stable, and who can be quickly integrated into the life of a church. We should also be aware that Jesus' death on the cross was the ultimate in problem-centred ministry. His death dealt with the root cause of suffering, by paying the penalty for sin and death. His death was ultimately part of his Father's plan to bring in a new creation, a creation where there shall be neither "mourning nor crying nor pain any more" (Rev 21:4).

This is not to say that there will be a quick fix. Anyone who understands the reality of the cross of Christ knows also that the problem of sin and suffering goes right through creation, and required the death of God-become-man to set it to rights. Anyone who lives in the world with their eyes open knows that the final day, where things are set to right, has not yet happened. Our solutions to the suffering of the world will only ever be partial until Jesus returns in triumph and judgement on that great day.

For this reason, the encouragements we offer can't be trivial and facile. Although our encouragement comes from God's word, there will be times when we ought simply to "weep with those who weep" (Rom 12:15).

For all this, the fact that we have been shaped by God's word means that we will have something to offer. Even the action of bringing dinner to those who need practical help is a good and important thing to do, and for Christians comes about because we've understood and been transformed by the command to "love your neighbour". Our careful and sensitive listening will fall into this category too, as will our patient persistence in what may be a difficult relationship. Often in the context of such a relationship there will be an opportunity to offer a word that is fitting, whether a word of comfort or a question that shows sensitivity to the situation, or a reminder of God's perspective. Even a fumbling word, spoken with compassion, is better than an embarrassed avoidance. If such words come with genuine love and humility, mistakes in speaking can be forgiven and overcome, and the relationship will be all the stronger for it. It may (or may not) help to read the Bible or pray with someone who is in grief or pain. Because it is true that "love covers a multitude of sins" (1 Pet 4:8), it is better to make a mistake in love and apologize, than not to act at all.

Romans 5:1-11, the book of Job, and Hebrews 12 are just some of many parts of the Bible that speak about how Christians can take comfort from God in the midst of suffering. The more we understand and are shaped by the Bible's perspective on suffering, the more we will have to offer those who are going through difficult times.[4]

Hard words

Sometimes a single hard word from a friend can have as much effect as a year's worth of Bible studies. I'm slightly embarrassed to admit that, when I was a university student, half of my normal conversation consisted of staggeringly well-remembered scripts from the TV show *Monty Python's Flying Circus*. I excuse myself only a little

---

[4]   Don Carson's *How Long, O Lord? Reflections on Suffering and Evil* (IVP, Leicester, 1990) deals helpfully with the subject of Christian suffering. It is not so much for the person in the midst of suffering, as for someone who is wanting to think about suffering biblically.

bit by pleading that it helped sharpen my memory for passing exams, and for remembering bits of the Bible to use in conversation.

It took the sharp rebuke of the member of one of my Bible study groups to make me realize that not everyone shared my love of *Python*; and that not everyone who shared my love of the show loved hearing it quoted when we swapped prayer points; and that there was at least one person (the one telling me off) who actually found it very annoying. For once, I resisted the almost unstoppable urge to respond with another Monty Python zinger from *The Argument* skit, or to perhaps quote the venerable *Dead Parrot* sketch, or even the less well-known but useful all-purpose rejoinder "society's to blame!"—you know, the one from the *Church Police* skit. I went away and thought about what this fellow Bible study group member had to say, all the while feeling somewhat embarrassed and annoyed.

But for all that, what he said that evening had a useful, permanent effect on the way that I thought about both Bible study groups and conversation, and how I ought to put the needs and concerns of others first.

If you have been rebuked you will know that it is an unpleasant experience that lodges in the memory and, when done by the right person at the right time, produces permanent change. Certainly that is why the writer of Proverbs says "faithful are the wounds of a friend" (Prov 27:6). The fact that it is unpleasant probably explains much of our reluctance to speak hard words. Still, obedience to the Bible's teaching and the desire to help others are both good reasons for persisting, and trying to get this right.

Matthew 18:15-20 sets the pattern. Jesus tells his disciples that if someone does something, "if your brother sins against you", you should try to fix it up privately. If that doesn't work, then one or two other people should join in and go to the brother, "that every charge may be established by the evidence of two or three witnesses". After that, it is a matter for the whole church.

There might be a few tricky questions about what this looks like in practice. Rebuking and disciplining someone is painful and difficult, and a lot of churches don't handle it very well. But still, it ought to be done, and the process ought to start with the person or people who are closest to the problem. If you are that close person, it's the easiest thing in the world to hope that someone else will deal with it. But if we take this idea seriously, it's better to assume that we ought to have first crack at dealing with a problem that is right there under our nose.

The Bible doesn't leave the questions of 'how' to our guesswork.[5] 2 Timothy 2:24-26, for example, says that we ought to be patient and gentle, hoping to produce repentance. What we are hoping is that the person we are speaking to (and possibly finding ourselves having to fight with) will be there in heaven with us on the final day, singing praise to Jesus.

---

[5]   Worth having a look at: Matt 23, 1 Cor 5:1-11, Gal 2:11, Gal 5:12, 2 John 10, and a number of other places which deal with those who openly reject the gospel. The ultimate aim is protection of believers and restoration of those who rebel. Silence is never an option.

If that's so, then maybe this is a time for praying to God for the courage to speak to someone about a hard subject. "Faithful are the wounds of a friend."

Things we write

You wouldn't expect a book on encouragement to conclude without some reference to what we write!

My grandmother was extremely shy and would often remain silent rather than offer an opinion. But she had the gift of writing wonderful Christmas cards that said a great deal with few words. Once or twice during my time working in student ministry, particular friends wrote letters to me. It wasn't often, and they weren't long letters, but they were significant in sustaining me in my work. I have kept some of those letters and notes, and occasionally refer to them when life is difficult.

All this is to say that something in written form can have a powerful impact, especially when it is clear that effort has been taken (for example, a handwritten note from a busy person). If your church is in the habit of inviting written feedback from the congregation through weekly comment slips, you could write down something you learned for which you are thankful.

In a similar vein but on a different scale, those who are tongue-tied and find it hard to express themselves quickly, or perhaps are unable to leave home, may be able to contribute by writing letters to local papers or sending e-mails or postcards to people that are supported by the church.

Have a go

Once we begin to consider possibilities, there is an incredible range of things that can be done by people who want to encourage others. If you know the gospel, you have everything you need to make a start, and to keep on going; in fact, the Bible tells us that we have been blessed in Christ "with every spiritual blessing in the heavenly places" (Eph 1:3). Sometimes, in the daily grind of living the Christian life, we can forget this. The basic message of this book is this: don't forget God's many blessings; instead, have a go at talking about them to others. Those blessings we have in Christ are incredible. We have even more to look forward to when we go to be with him forever. In the meantime, that powerful word of the gospel that saved and blessed us is something we can use to save and bless others. Go on, have a go! And may God encourage you as you seek to encourage others.

> As each has received a gift, use it to serve one another, as good stewards of God's varied grace: whoever speaks, as one who speaks oracles of God; whoever serves, as one who serves by the strength that God supplies—in order that in everything God may be glorified through Jesus Christ. To him be glory and dominion for ever and ever. Amen. (1 Pet 4:10-11)

Chapter 10

THE END OF ENCOURAGEMENT

ONE OF THE MORE SURPRISING things we learn about encouragement in the Bible is that a day is coming when we will stop doing it, forever. Encouragement will cease, because it will no longer be needed. When that day comes, further encouragement will be a bit like shouting "Run faster! You're doing well!" to an athlete who has just won the race of his life—nice, but redundant, and it would have been useful earlier.

Let's recall the definition of Christian encouragement that we began with back in Chapter 1. At the beginning we said that Christian encouragement means speaking the truth in love, **as we wait for the day of judgement**.

Now when that day of judgement comes, we will have reached the goal of all our encouragement. That day will likewise spell the end of all **dis**couragement, of every regret and disappointment, sorrow, sadness, wickedness and evil. God himself will be our encourager on that day:

> And I heard a loud voice from the throne saying,
> "Behold, the dwelling place of God is with man. He
> will dwell with them, and they will be his people, and
> God himself will be with them as their God. He will
> wipe away every tear from their eyes, and death shall
> be no more, neither shall there be mourning nor
> crying nor pain anymore, for the former things have
> passed away." (Rev 21:3-4)

Indeed, the very heart of the encouragement we have to offer is the news that this day is coming. In the book of Revelation, the angel of God preaches this "eternal gospel": "Fear God and give him glory, because the hour of his judgement has come, and worship him who made heaven and earth, the sea and the springs of water" (Rev 14:7).

On that final day, God will be seen for who God is. Evil will come to an end. We will worship and serve him as we ought, and as we have always wanted to. It will be a fearful and terrifying day for those who haven't put their trust in Jesus. But for those who have loved and trusted Jesus as Lord, it is the day when everything we have hoped for comes to completion and finality, and the basis and content of our encouragement will be shown to be true for all eternity.

Judgement, therefore, is the thing that ultimately shapes our encouragement. No wonder that Jesus warns his hearers: "I tell you, on the day of judgement people will give account for every careless word they speak" (Matt 12:36).

The other side of this warning is that what we now do and say as Christians will have eternal value. It makes every encouraging word we say both indispensable and irreplaceable. Once we start to see this—and if we understand the gospel, we already know it—nothing can ever be the same. Our values, our speaking, our whole way of looking at the things that matter will be the complete opposite of what the world expects:

> For the word of the cross is folly to those who are
> perishing, but to us who are being saved it is the power
> of God ... we preach Christ crucified, a stumbling block
> to Jews and folly to Gentiles, but to those who are
> called, both Jews and Greeks, Christ the power of God
> and the wisdom of God. (1 Cor 1:18, 23-24)

Because of all this—because of the cross, and because of the coming day of judgement—turning up at church will actually matter to us. In the brief time we have on earth, we ought to work out how to stir one another up to love and good works—"not neglecting to meet together", as the writer of Hebrews puts it, "but **encouraging** one another, and all the more as you see the Day drawing near" (Heb 10:25). For those who trust in the cross and know that the Day is approaching, spending time building relationships and speaking the truth in love to others will assume new significance—as opposed to saving for holidays, paying off mortgages, or looking after our bodies with material things. There is more to life than a lazy, early retirement funded by a large pension payout. Why? Because seeing our fellow believers standing firm on the day of judgement will matter to us more than anything, as it matters to God. In encouraging each other to stand firm, we will be sharing the purpose for which Christ died and rose again:

> ... Christ loved the church and gave himself up for her, that he might sanctify her, having cleansed her by the washing of water with the word, so that he might present the church to himself in splendour, without spot or wrinkle or any such thing, that she might be holy and without blemish. (Eph 5:25-27)

Thus, we offer encouragement to each other for a brief time now, in order that we may be joined to Christ and share his majesty on the final day.

> For our light and momentary troubles are achieving for us an eternal glory that far outweighs them all. So we fix our eyes not on what is seen, but on what is unseen. For what is seen is temporary, but what is unseen is eternal. (2 Cor 4:17-18, NIV)

IN WRITING THIS BOOK my mind has often drifted to my good friend Jack, now gone to glory, the eighty-year-old who met me at church on my first visit and told me his testimony to God's goodness. He was part of a small group of lovely men and women in their 70s and 80s who were faithfully getting on with praying and befriending and supporting the work of the church. One of them said to me, "We don't find all these changes at church easy, but if it's going to help the young people, then we want to support it". They gave money to help gospel proclamation. They were generous with their time and energy. They had retired from work. But they hadn't retired from living as Christians, and their efforts in gospel service put many of the young wealthy workaholics in our church to shame. The young ones were working to shore up mortgage payments in a wealthy suburb. The old ones were working for eternity.

Like those older friends, the more we remember that judgement is coming, the more we will want to encourage people to be ready for it. Everything else we put our effort into in this life is temporary; everything will fail at the Lord's return. Houses and mortgages and university degrees will all disappear.

> But the day of the Lord will come like a thief, and then the heavens will pass away with a roar, and the heavenly bodies will be burned up and dissolved, and the earth and the works that are done on it will be exposed. (2 Pet 3:10)

To work at encouraging others we are in relationship with, and to do this as Christians, is to build a work that lasts into eternity. Our words of encouragement are helping people to live with Jesus Christ as Lord, preparing for the day when we will share in his rule over all creation through the resurrection of the body. This is the work of the Lord, and as Paul encourages us, when we do it we know that "in the Lord your labour is not in vain" (1 Cor 15:58).

Another man who popped into my mind as I wrote is Alvin, one of those slightly unusual people that every healthy church seems to attract. Indeed, if there are no slightly awkward people in our congregations, it suggests that something has gone wrong with our understanding of the gospel—because we don't know how to welcome people that Jesus loves.

There are ways in which Alvin, by his dress, conversation and appearance, shows that he is not socially aware. In almost every conversation I've had with Alvin since the time I met him (the ones where he hasn't slightly obsessively complained about the poor quality of the PowerPoint presentation and use of the overhead projector), he has mentioned one, two, three, four or five people that he happened to be evangelizing at the time. They were not the same people each time, and they were not invented, and they seemed to be rising stars in their chosen area of expertise.

Behind his obvious disadvantages, Alvin has latched hold of the gospel of coming judgement and divine grace. Because he is not easily embarrassed, and because he doesn't even seem to understand how to exploit his relationships for personal gain, people who have almost no natural interest in Jesus will hear him out, and will ask him questions about God that they might feel embarrassed about asking anyone else.

If you have understood the gospel of coming judgement and divine grace, then you too have an eternal message that you can use to bring encouragement, forgiveness and eternal life to believer and unbeliever alike. Don't hold back, and don't consider your own limitations. Speak this word of hope to anyone who will give you half a chance.

Appendix

DISCUSSION GUIDE

THE QUESTIONS THAT FOLLOW are designed to make it easy for small groups to discuss the content of *Encouragement: How Words Change Lives* with their Bibles open. Feel free to pick and choose your way through the questions (and references) depending on how much time you have available.

You can work through the discussion guide one chapter per session (10 sessions) or by combining some of the chapters as follows (6 sessions):

i.   chapters 1 and 2
ii. chapter 3
iii. chapters 4 and 5
iv. chapters 6 and 7
v.   chapter 8
vi. chapters 9 and 10

Chapter 1: What Christian encouragement is

1. Look at Ephesians 4:11-16. What does this passage say about the what and how of Christian encouragement?

2. Look at Hebrews 10:19-25. What does this passage say about the what and how of Christian encouragement?

3. Now look at the definition of Christian encouragement in the box on page 11. In the light of the passages you've read, how would you change or improve it?

4. How have words changed your life, for better or for worse?

Chapter 2: The power of words

1. "Sticks and stones may break my bones, but names will never hurt me." Think of ways in which experience or the Bible contradict this saying. You may like to refer to the table of verses from Proverbs in this chapter (pp. 19-20).

2. Look at Romans 3:9-20.
   a. What do the verses say about the way we normally use words?
   b. What does this show about what we're like?
   c. What do we deserve from God? (Compare Rom 6:23.)

3. Summarize what it was that you believed when you became a Christian (i.e. the gospel).
   a. How does the gospel bring you from death to life?
   b. How could your words bring someone from death to life? What is your role in the process?

Chapter 3: The greatest speaker

1. Look at the following examples of how God speaks. Taking into account the story of the whole Bible, what do we see God's words achieving?

   Gen 1, 2:15-17, 3:14-19, 9:11, 12:1-3; Isa 55:10-11; Rom 4:17; 2 Cor 4:6; 1 Thess 4:15-18.

2. What do we learn about the nature and power of God's words from these passages?

3. Skim-read Proverbs 12, and take note of what is said about words. How and why can our words be like God's?

Chapter 4: How Christian encouragement works—Part I

1. What part did words play in you becoming a Christian?

2. Read 1 Thessalonians 1.

   a. What happened when the Thessalonians heard the gospel?

   b. How did it happen that the gospel went out from the Thessalonians?

3. What role do our words play in God's plan? (Compare Eph 4:11-16.)

4. How would you apply 1 Thessalonians 1 and Ephesians 4:11-16 to your own situation?

Chapter 5: How Christian encouragement works — Part II

1. Read Proverbs 8. How do we get wisdom? (Compare Prov 9:10.)

2. Read 1 Corinthians 1:18-2:5. According to this passage, where do we find true wisdom?

3. What is the role of prayer in finding wisdom? (Compare Jas 1:5-8.)

4. Compare God's wisdom with the world's wisdom. How are they the same? How are they different?

Chapter 6: Speaking up

1. Look at Acts 20:17-21 and 1 Corinthians 2:2-5. What can you discover about what and how Paul taught his hearers?

2. Look at 1 Corinthians 9:19-23. What can you discover about Paul's methods?

3. What can we learn from Paul's message, motivation and method?

4. A friend says, "We've just suffered a miscarriage". How would Paul's example would help us speak to this person about suffering?

Chapter 7: How we say what we say

1. A friend says, "I'm struggling with a temptation to look at pornography". Think of how your advice could be gracious rather than legalistic.

2. What things will help you to be able to offer specific advice to someone?

3. What will help you to be a good listener?

4. Considering the list of suggestions for 'how we say what we say' in this chapter, what other ideas can you think of? What do you need to work on in this area?

Chapter 8: Is God's word changing you?

1. Look at Isaiah 1:12-17. What is the nature of true religion? (Compare Jas 1:27.)

2. How can the quality of our lives have an effect for the gospel? (Compare Rom 2:24; 1 Pet 2:13-15; 1 Tim 4:16.)

3. What dangers are there, for us and for others, if our lives are inconsistent with the gospel?

4. What will help us to live consistently with the gospel?

Chapter 9: Making a start

1. Look at 1 Corinthians 12. What does this tell us about the what, why and how of starting to encourage other people?

2. Look at the suggestions for how to encourage others that are given in this chapter. Which of these are you doing? Which could you start to do?

3. How could you help others to be encouragers too?

4. According to 1 Peter 4:10-11, what's the motivation for encouragement? How can we stop our encouragement of others from becoming legalistic or burdensome?

Chapter 10: The end of encouragement

1. How often do you talk or pray about judgement with other Christians?

2. According to Hebrews 10:19-25, why is the idea of judgement important for Christian life and encouragement?

3. According to 2 Peter 3:8-13, what's the connection between judgement and the way we live now?

4. How can we help each other to think about the day of judgement?

matthiasmedia

Matthias Media is a ministry team of like-minded, evangelical Christians working together to achieve a particular goal, as summarized in our mission statement:

> *To serve our Lord Jesus Christ, and the growth of his gospel in the world, by producing and delivering high quality, Bible-based resources.*

It was in 1988 that we first started pursuing this mission together, and in God's kindness we now have more than 250 different ministry resources being distributed all over the world. These resources range from Bible studies and books, through to training courses and audio sermons.

To find out more about our large range of very useful products, and to access samples and free downloads, visit our website:

www.matthiasmedia.com.au

How to buy our resources

1. Direct from us over the internet:
   – in the US: www.matthiasmedia.com
   – in Australia and the rest of the world: www.matthiasmedia.com.au

2. Direct from us by phone:
   – in the US: 1 866 407 4530
   – in Australia: 1800 814 360 (Sydney: 9663 1478)
   – international: +61-2-9663-1478

3. Through a range of outlets in various parts of the world. Visit **www.matthiasmedia.com.au/international.php** for details about recommended retailers in your part of the world, including www.thegoodbook.co.uk in the United Kingdom.

4. Trade enquiries can be addressed to:
   – in the US: sales@matthiasmedia.com
   – in the UK: sales@ivpbooks.com
   – in Australia and the rest of the world: sales@matthiasmedia.com.au

Also by Gordon Cheng ...

Six Steps to Encouragement

God has given every Christian an enormous privilege and gift: the power to speak his life-changing word into the lives of other people. There's no reason at all for there to be 'passengers' in a church: every Christian can change the lives of those around them through knowing and telling the message of God's grace, whether in front of a group, in a handwritten note, in a one-to-one conversation over morning tea, or in a thousand other ways. Every Christian can be a channel of encouragement.

In *Six Steps to Encouragement*, you'll learn the why and how of personal encouragement. Through video input, Bible study, practical examples, discussions and hands-on exercises, you'll discover how to bring life, hope and strength to those around you by bringing the powerful word of God to them. You'll also work through practical case studies such as welcoming newcomers, listening, rebuking, and dealing with suffering.

Six Steps to Encouragement is a six-session course, ideal for:

- Training all leaders in church
- Home group Bible studies
- Welcoming committee
- Everyone who wants to be a channel of encouragement

To run the course you will need a workbook for each person (which also contains notes for group leaders), and the DVD or video to use in the group.

FOR MORE INFORMATION OR TO ORDER CONTACT:

Matthias Media	**Matthias Media (USA)**
Telephone: +61-2-9663-1478	Telephone: 1-866-407-4530
Facsimile: +61-2-9663-3265	Facsimile: 724-964-8166
Email: sales@matthiasmedia.com.au	Email: sales@matthiasmedia.com
www.matthiasmedia.com.au	www.matthiasmedia.com

A Sinner's Guide to Holiness

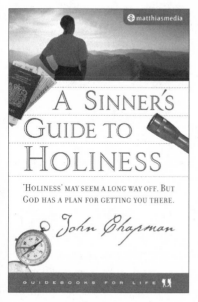

What is holiness? Why do I need it? And why is it such a struggle for me to achieve holiness in my everyday life?

In *A Sinner's Guide to Holiness*, well-known evangelist John Chapman explores what the Bible has to say about holiness—where it begins, how it makes progress in our lives, and its ultimate fulfilment as we are changed into Christ's glorious likeness on the Last Day.

This book is a timely publication in this day and age, when we have often lost sight of the holiness of God. And when we do, it seems like an impossible task to achieve our own holiness. But John Chapman tells us that becoming holy is a vital, worthwhile goal for every Christian.

FOR MORE INFORMATION OR TO ORDER CONTACT:

Matthias Media
Telephone: +61-2-9663-1478
Facsimile: +61-2-9663-3265
Email: sales@matthiasmedia.com.au
www.matthiasmedia.com.au

Matthias Media (USA)
Telephone: 1-866-407-4530
Facsimile: 724-964-8166
Email: sales@matthiasmedia.com
www.matthiasmedia.com

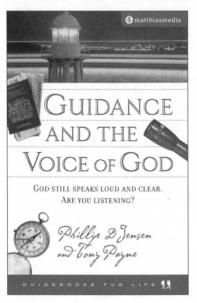

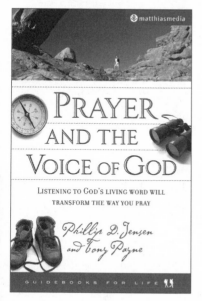

Faith

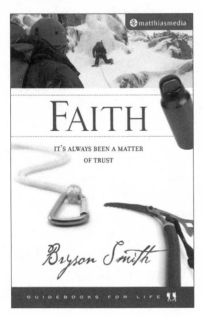

Everyone knows that faith is central to the Christian life. But what is 'faith'? What makes it so important? What are we meant to have faith in, and what difference should our faith make to everyday life?

In six short chapters, Bryson Smith takes us on a climb—a climb to look out at the magnificent wisdom of God and understand faith in all its glory. In the course of this journey, we start to grasp what a life of faith looks like and why faith is more precious than gold.

FOR MORE INFORMATION OR TO ORDER CONTACT:

Matthias Media
Telephone: +61-2-9663-1478
Facsimile: +61-2-9663-3265
Email: sales@matthiasmedia.com.au
www.matthiasmedia.com.au

Matthias Media (USA)
Telephone: 1-866-407-4530
Facsimile: 724-964-8166
Email: sales@matthiasmedia.com
www.matthiasmedia.com